Advance Pr

How to Start a Busine
– Second Edition

Laura Brandenburg has been involved with helping people become business analysts for years. As you read *How to Start a Business Analyst Career*, you feel that she is talking directly to you, listening to your travails, and offering solid, practical, and applicable advice. There is no pie-in-the-sky theories about how things should be, just **simple, usable, honest, real-world descriptions of the way things actually are in the world of business analysis.**

How to Start a Business Analyst Career is the touchstone for all readers wishing to enter the profession of business analysis. Laura uses the wonderful artifice of *a day in the life of a business analyst* to demonstrate what someone anticipating a business analyst career might experience in a normal day's activities. Certainly after reading Chapter 1, a prospective business analyst will have an idea of whether the job is what they imagined it to be.

Then Laura uses the *day in the life* as a reference point to discuss the various aspects of being a business analyst: what knowledge, skills, and abilities are needed to be successful as a business analyst, how to use your current experience as you begin your business analyst career and how to gain relevant business analyst experience without being a business analyst, how to determine which of the many business analyst roles is right for you, and much more.

I recommend *How to Start a Business Analyst Career* to anyone who is considering becoming a business analyst, anyone who wishes to change their career to business analysis, any business analyst who wants to get a refresher on the profession, and any older business analyst who desires to read a bit of nostalgia for the early days of their career.

~ Steve Blais, author of *Business Analysis: Best Practices for Success*

Starting a business analysis career is not an easy feat. Having mentored and coached a number of professionals interested in breaking into a business analysis career, I know that for most people it takes a lot of focus and perseverance to get there. Laura's book provides spot-on recommendations to help you drastically reduce the amount of effort and time required to jump-start your business analyst career. **If you were to invest in just one resource to help you transition into a high-paying and rewarding business analyst career, you couldn't do better than this book.**

~ Adriana Beal, Product Manager and
Principal Consultant at Beal Projects LLC

Laura has had a single-minded focus on helping new business analysts enter the profession for several years. When people ask me, *how do I become a business analyst?*, I always sigh (inside!) because I would love to give them a simple guide, but I know that it is complicated, and any answer has to start with *it depends...*

Laura has done the almost impossible by providing a route into business analysis via a step-by-step process that anyone can follow.

She has done a great service for the want-to-be business analysis community.

~ Alex Papworth, Business Analyst and Mentor, BAmentor.com

I have often said that I did not choose my career as a business analyst, but that it chose me over many years of trial and error. Having said that, if I had been in the possession of this book so many years ago to help me make an informed career decision, I likely would have chosen business analysis as a career.

Let's face it, most of us do not have the luxury of being independently wealthy, let alone have career opportunities that actually match what we went to school for. As our careers progress, most of us travel from job to job hoping that the next move we make will feel right or that it will fill a missing void in our lives. Did you know what you wanted to be when you grew up? Do you find yourself fulfilling that dream today? Wouldn't it be great to make an informed career decision for a change?

What a wonderful gift you can give yourself with this book, which will help you decide if business analysis is the right career move for you. The world needs a lot more business analysts. *How to Start a Business Analyst Career* will guide you, or someone you know, on your journey to becoming a business analyst.

Enjoy the read, and best of luck on your future business analysis career!

~ Bob the BA (aka Bob Prentiss)

Professionals across the globe are looking for opportunities in the field of business analysis to grow and revitalize their careers. In *How to Start a Business Analyst Career*, Laura Brandenburg combines her deep working knowledge of business analysis with a passion for assisting aspiring business analysts to provide an excellent resource for identifying and navigating the path to a successful business analysis career. **Practical, principle-based, and easy to read and use**, professionals of any background or career level seeking an opportunity in business analysis stand to benefit from this book.

~ Jonathan Babcock, Jabian Consulting and
Editor of PracticalAnalyst.com

This newest installment of Laura Brandenburg's books about starting and advancing your business analysis career will help not only those contemplating a business analysis career but also those young in their business analysis career to catapult their career to greater heights. This is a testament to Laura's expertise and passion for business analysis and helping others advance their career in business analysis.

Laura uses the *Guide to the Business Analysis Body of Knowledge® (BABOK®)*, the Business Analysis Competency Model, and more than a decade of experience to assist others in their understanding of what business analysts do and how to build a successful business analysis career. **This book helps you understand how to use your experience in other business areas to transition into business analysis above entry-level positions.** It not only describes how to develop your individual strategy to transition your career into business analysis, it describes as well how to stay current with trends in the business analysis space by connecting with others in the profession and leveraging those relationships to advance your career.

I highly recommend this book for those interested in a business analysis career and those wishing to take their career to new places. I am confident that you will find it a valuable resource.

~ Aaron Whittenberger, CBAP, Regional Director
of America's Eastern Region, International
Institute of Business Analysis (IIBA®)

How to Start a Business Analyst Career

Second Edition

The handbook to apply business analysis techniques, select requirements training, and explore job roles leading to a lucrative technology career

Laura Brandenburg, CBAP

Foreword by
Ellen Gottesdiener

How to Start a Business Analyst Career: The handbook to apply business analysis techniques, select requirements training, and explore job roles leading to a lucrative technology career
by Laura Brandenburg, CBAP

ISBN: 978-0-9838611-2-6
Library of Congress Cataloging in Publication Data

Published by Clear Spring Business Analysis LLC
The parent company of Bridging the Gap

Second Edition

Printed in the United States of America

To my two daughters, who will inherit the world we create
and make it even better.

Contents

Foreword

Over the past several years, I have worked with all types of clients, and I've noticed a pattern. Increasingly, they—like most organizations—need faster product delivery, desire super-efficient practices, and, above all, pursue a relentless goal of providing value to the customer. At the same time, they face a host of practical problems.

First, products are complex and therefore expensive to build and maintain.

Second, customers are getting more savvy and demanding.

Third, requirements risks continue to be the most insidious challenge in any development effort.

And then there is the fourth practical problem—people.

Products are discovered and delivered by teams of human beings whose best work emerges from healthy collaboration. But that doesn't happen spontaneously. People need to learn how to systematically plan and analyze the product at a high level while at the same time drilling down to the details.

A core element of these problems is the need to specify product requirements, the basis for development and delivery. While technologies get better and better, requirements remain a conundrum—they are necessary to know but wickedly difficult to obtain and agree on. Requirements will always be, to paraphrase Fred Brooks, the most difficult part of any development effort.

Living in the heart of this challenge are the professionals who function as business analysts. To help organizations respond to these challenges, I have authored three books: *Requirements by Collaboration: Workshops for Defining Needs, The Software Requirements Memory Jogger*, and most recently *Discover to Deliver: Agile Product Planning and Analysis* with Mary Gorman. Additionally, as founder and Principle of EBG Consulting, I have worked with global clients and spoken at numerous industry conferences, putting me in contact with hundreds of professionals in business analysis and related disciplines.

I have participated as an expert reviewer for the International Institute of Business Analysis (IIBA) *Business Analysis Body of Knowledge®* (*BABOK®*) and as a reviewer of the PMI® Business Analysis Practice Guide. I have also been a member of the committee building the Agile Extension of the BABOK, the IIBA® Endorsed Education Provider committee, the executive steering committee overseeing what became the Project Management Institute Professional in Business Analysis (PMI-PBA℠) designation, and I have been a board member of the International Requirements Engineering Board® (IREB).

Through all of this, what I have observed time and time again is that to be a great business analyst you need a high tolerance for ambiguity and a concurrent drive for specificity.

While business analysis is much better known as a profession than in years past and you have many resources to support you in succeeding in your work, the path to becoming a business analyst and thriving in a business analyst career is not clear cut. Consider *How to Start a Business Analyst Career* your guidebook to finding your best path forward in the profession.

The first edition sold thousands of copies. Now author Laura Brandenburg has revised and updated the book to educate readers about recent changes that impact the profession. Examples include the introduction of the CCBA® and PMI's PBA℠ and the expansion of roles in the job marketplace requiring business analysis competencies. The book you are holding in your hands (or on your e-book reading device) is the most comprehensive guide available for creating an actionable plan that enables you to start a business analyst career.

Laura Brandenburg and I initially connected in 2009, spoke on the phone several times, shared each other's work online, and finally met in person at the Building Business Capability Conference in 2013. She is known within the business analysis community as a leader in helping talented mid-career professionals successfully start careers in business analysis. What I like most about her writing is how accessible the material is. Reading this book is like chatting with a trusted friend, one who offers you practical advice in an intimate yet professional way.

Her advice ranges from finding a job, to considerations for telecommuting, to your involvement in decision-making. Though her focus is on getting started in the role of business analyst, the solid foundation she recommends is easy to build on and could lead to many future roles, such as coach, consultant, product owner, and product or project manager.

Key Elements To Note: Upon reading this book and working through the Putting It To Practice exercises, you'll find that:

You become well versed in what a business analyst does, how your days will flow, and how your skills will be leveraged. I'm honored that Laura incorporated my suggestion to include a real sample work day that illustrates many of the less tangible skills that business analysts need to be successful in their work.

You already possess more relevant experience than you might think, which may expand the possibilities open to you within the business analysis profession.

You are able to apply business analysis techniques right now, using one of the many ideas Laura suggests in Chapter 3.

You are guided by Laura's descriptions of the most common types of business analyst roles rather than perplexed by the array of skills and experiences required by today's job descriptions.

You are ready to take action and make your career goals a reality using straightforward planning techniques and momentum-building strategies.

I enjoyed Laura's story about the roses in Chapter 2 and the accompanying reminder to pay attention to what is in front of you, especially to your own strengths. I also appreciated the questions she has interspersed throughout the book.

Laura's style and stories reflect two of the biggest skills every business analyst should develop: The best analysts are a) great observers and b) ask really good questions, from a place of genuine curiosity, using the *beginner's mind* (http://en.wikipedia.org/wiki/Shoshin).

Don't miss Chapter 4's Pay It Forward. It isn't just good advice, it's good karma. You might also want to pay close attention to Laura's excellent interview advice and her emphasis on the importance of getting involved, going to events, and connecting. In our digital world, it is more important than ever to add a personal touch to your job search and to your day-to-day work.

I highly recommend *How to Start a Business Analyst Career* to any professional looking to get their start in a business analysis career. If you are a project manager, software developer, technical writer, business subject matter expert, quality assurance professional, or otherwise employed and interested in business analysis, this is the first book you should pick up as you begin your journey.

The book is particularly relevant for those who have been in the workforce for at least a few years, as you will most likely find that you have related experience to draw from. Don't worry if you currently think that that is not the case. Laura walks you through exactly how to appraise your own experience and your skills.

Although the book focuses on the business analyst role in the context of a software project, a technical background is not necessary to be successful. In reading the book, you will discover ways to learn more about the technical concepts you need to know to have a rewarding and prosperous career as a business analyst.

Read it. Enjoy it. Benefit from it.

With Warm Regards,

~ ellen

November 2014

Ellen Gottesdiener

President/Founder, EBG Consulting

www.ebgconsulting.com | www.DiscoverToDeliver.com

@ellengott | https://www.linkedin.com/in/ellengottesdiener

Introduction

Since I began writing about business analysis more than five years ago, the most common question I am asked is about getting started in the business analysis profession. The path is not clear cut. No degree will guarantee that you will find employment in a business analyst role. No one job pre-qualifies you to become a business analyst. No matter what you see in the job postings, technology experience is not undeniably required nor is expertise in a specific business domain. What is more, few junior-level business analyst jobs exist, and they are reserved for recent college graduates willing to accept entry-level salaries.

Yet, every year professionals with experience in other occupations begin careers in business analysis. They do not start at the bottom, however. They jump right in at the middle and sometimes move directly into senior-level roles.

With the average salary for a business analyst in the United States reaching above $90,000 per year[1], we are seeing more and more talented, experienced professionals pursue business analyst jobs. It is not uncommon for a senior-level business analyst to earn a six-figure salary, and consultants, team leads, and managers do even better. You will frequently find business analysis toward the top of hot-job lists, albeit commonly under other titles such as Systems Analyst, Management Consultant, and Process Analyst. Whatever you decide to call us, it is clear that business analysis is becoming a profitable and sought-after profession.

I am excited to see this because I think we need the best of the best performing business analysis. The best of the best does not necessarily mean someone with the most meticulous process or the finest modeling

---

[1] http://www.bridging-the-gap.com/business-analyst-salary/

skills. It does mean that you are a strong communicator, problem solver, and collaborator. It does mean that you have an inner drive to get things done and to be sure that those things add concrete value to your organization. The best of the best come from all areas of expertise and all different kinds of jobs, but they find their home in business analysis.

My promise to you is that this book will help you find your best path to a business analysis career. You may be wondering if this is the right career choice, if you have what it takes to be a business analyst, and what you can do to maximize your opportunities. After reading this book and working through the Putting It To Practice exercises, you will have concrete answers to these questions. More than that, you will know exactly what to do next to move forward in your business analysis career.

The first edition of this book, published in 2009, helped thousands of readers carve their path into the business analysis profession. Since authoring the first edition, I've helped numerous coaching clients and course participants apply the principles laid out in the book and, in doing so, discovered ways to clarify the recommendations. Besides, there have been important changes in the profession to consider. This second edition has been completely updated and reorganized to ensure that you receive a comprehensive handbook that will help you create an actionable plan for starting your business analyst career.

This book is geared mostly toward business analysts in the information technology space. In this sense, the term business analyst is used to identify individuals who facilitate requirements and organizational improvements as part of delivering software solutions and the corresponding updates to business processes. The role of the business analyst is and can be much broader than this, but the vast majority of jobs directly aligned to the business analysis profession are found in this space.

The best way to use this book is to read it from beginning to end and to invest time in each of the Putting It To Practice exercises. You may find it easier to read the entire book once and then circle back through to do the exercises. The chapters and sections are organized in a logical progression, beginning with learning about the business analysis profession and the skills required, then how to create opportunities, and finally how to develop a career strategy to achieve the forward momentum that you want from your career.

Each chapter contains exercises that help you act on what you learn. You will benefit the most if you take the time to do a fair number of the exercises that involve thinking, writing, self-assessment, self-reflection, and research. The exercises are not designed to be busywork. You are too busy for that. Instead, they are designed to help you gain the insights you need to make the best possible use of your time and financial resources as you commence your business analyst career.

While all of the information you need to complete each exercise is included, some of the exercises are supported by worksheets that are included in a Resource Pack for this book. The worksheets make the work a little easier by providing template forms that you may use to complete the exercise. You will receive a link to download the Resource Pack for free inside the book.

Before diving in, get a notebook or open a file folder on your computer in which to store the information that you will collect and the writing that you will do as part of each exercise.

Thank you for investing in this book and allowing me to share this journey with you.

Let's get started.

✓ Putting It To Practice #1

Take The Business Analysis Litmus Test

This exercise will help you explore whether business analysis is a suitable career choice for you. You can take this test in any way you like. I suggest writing a few sentences in your notebook or in a document saved in your file folder on your computer to respond to each question.

1. Do you frequently find yourself in meetings? If so, do you like them? What do you like about the meetings you do attend? If you don't like them, why?
2. How do you deal with situations where people are clearly not communicating? Do you naturally find yourself paraphrasing others in order to help them communicate?
3. Do you like to write? Is your writing precise and clear?
4. Are you comfortable working independently at your desk or computer for between two and three hours at a time?
5. When you use a new tool or website, do you think of ways to make it better?
6. In situations of conflict, do you find that you can maintain a neutral or at least a balanced position and see both sides of the argument?

7. Are you comfortable drawing on a white board? Do you get excited about seeing people align around a concept or idea?

8. Do you find yourself intuitively understanding new systems or processes and dissecting the rules that make them work? Are you driven to understand why things work the way they do?

9. Would you say that you have a thorough understanding of the organizations of which you have been a part? Do you know who is responsible for what and how things are accomplished? (Examples could include a community organization, an educational institution, a club, or a company.)

10. Do you tend to enjoy the early part of projects, when there are a lot of ideas, possibility, and uncertainty? Do you like to help drive more clarity and concreteness as you transform the realm of possibility into what actually will get done?

11. Do you like to ask questions? Do you seem to have a knack for asking the right question at the right time?

12. Do people at work confide in you? Do people at work come to you to help them think through a problem or make a decision?

13. Do you like to solve problems? Especially the really tough ones? Do you see these as occasions to strut your mental prowess and not as annoyances?

14. Do you enjoy learning? Do you pick up new skills and techniques quickly?
15. Do you like to support collaboration between the people you work with? Do you get more people involved in problems and solutions instead of fewer?

If you can answer yes to most of the above questions, business analysis may be a career in which you would find fulfillment. It is not a guarantee. This is not a scientific test. But it is based on my personal experience, what I love about the role, and my discussions with other business analysts who are happy with their career choice.

If you cannot answer yes to most of these questions, this might not be the right career choice for you. But it also may mean that you lack some of the prerequisite professional experience to really know for sure. You will benefit from reading a few more chapters to explore the profession in more depth.

CHAPTER 1

What It's Like To Be A Business Analyst

I like the fact that business analysis work does not change as fast as software development but that I am continuously learning.
~ Doug Goldberg, Senior Business Analyst

Business Analysis Defined

Business analysts solve problems for organizations. While the set of activities, responsibilities, and qualifications varies widely among business analyst jobs, business analysts are always responsible for leading change, creating clarity, and driving alignment.

According to the *Business Analysis Body of Knowledge (BABOK) Guide® Version 3*:

> *Business analysis ultimately helps organizations to understand the needs of the enterprise and why they want to create change, design possible solutions, and describe how those solutions can deliver value.*[2]

Business analysts work on all types of projects and change efforts. Some of the more widespread applications of business analysis activities include software changes, business process improvements, and ensuring compliance with regulations.

---

[2] Draft accessed via IIBA website during open review period in June 2014. Version 3 may not be accessed until publication, anticipated in April 2015.

When thinking about what business analysts do, it may be helpful to think about the concept of change in the broadest possible sense. Business analysis techniques can be applied to any scale of change, from large to small. A large change could take a year or more to design, implement, and deploy. One example would be to build a strategy for integrating a newly acquired business unit. Another type of large change would be the deployment of a new software system that impacts many business process areas. A small change, on the other hand, may be completed in as little as a day or a week. Updating a field on one user interface screen or producing a new report from existing data would be examples of relatively small changes.

Regardless of the scale of the change, the business analyst works with stakeholders across the organization to understand the business objectives driving the change, define the scope of the change, analyze and specify the detailed requirements related to the change, and finally, support the implementation of the change.

While business analysts have historically been referred to as the bridge between the business and the information technology groups, the reality is much more multi-faceted. Business analysts bridge knowledge, perspective, and understanding gaps between stakeholders from different functional departments and levels of the organization. A stakeholder is anyone who has an interest in the change or influence over the change. Stakeholders may be on the receiving end of the change or part of implementing the change.

It is not uncommon for a business analyst to gain approval from a director-level sponsor, discover information about how the process works from business users across several functional departments, negotiate technical possibilities with a technology architect, and communicate requirements to a developer and quality assurance engineer. A business analyst bridges multiple different gaps in understanding among all stakeholders to gain alignment on the go-forward plan and ensure that the implemented change generates as much value as possible.

The primary outputs of business analysis activities are requirements, which are packaged together in documents called specifications. A requirement is a condition or capability needed by a stakeholder to solve a problem or achieve an objective. A requirements specification includes the requirements specific to a change, a project, or a project component. Business analysts validate that the requirements are clear, complete, and represent stakeholder needs.

Business analysts employ an array of techniques to complete their work, and we will talk about the most common of them in Chapter 2. At the end of the day, the business analyst is responsible for attaining a shared understanding of what is to be achieved and helping stakeholders discover the best solution to deliver the most value to their organizations.

Before we take a deep dive into the skills required to be a business analyst, let's consider what it is like to be a business analyst. Decisions become easier if we can see and feel what the end result will be like. The remainder of this chapter is intended to help you see yourself in a business analyst's shoes. I invite you to absorb what is written here and see yourself in different aspects of the role.

First, let's take a glimpse at a hypothetical real work day that a business analyst might experience.

A Real Work Day

It's Tuesday. I arrive at work at 8:45 a.m. I really wanted to make it in by 8:15, but there was an accident on the freeway that delayed me.

Before I left yesterday, my manager asked for feedback on some new projects. She wanted me to provide estimates and assumptions for planning purposes. I open up the document that she sent and see

[3] *Business Analysis Body of Knowledge*, Version 2.0. Page 230.

that it includes three projects. I read through the details. I can see immediately that one is simple. In fact, it was an idea that came up in one of my project meetings. The other two are new to me, and I have lots of questions. She needs the estimates by the end of the day. I go to her desk, and she's not there. I decide to send her an e-mail.

I click into my e-mail. In comes a flood of messages. At least ten contain the same subject line, and the chain was kicked off by the architect on my primary project. I read the last in the string hoping to follow the thread so I can respond before my 10:00 a.m. meeting. I see that the team is confused about the requirements but also about a new technical issue that hasn't been discussed. I reluctantly hit Reply All and let everyone know that I will schedule a meeting for later today or early tomorrow to discuss the issue.

The project manager on one of my minor projects visits my desk to ask what is driving a requirement. The implementation team is struggling to meet the deadline, and the project manager would like to propose that this particular requirement be deferred. I am able to clarify why it is important, but I think that there could be other ways to scale back and meet the deadline. He agrees to schedule a meeting for Wednesday or Thursday so we can go through the outstanding requirements and project timeline and put together a proposal to present to the business.

Now it is 9:30 and time to prepare for my 10:00 meeting. I print out the documents that we will be reviewing and give them a final glance. I write a few questions down, grab my notebook and laptop, and head to the conference room. Luckily, the previous meeting attendees are filing out a few minutes early. I fire up my laptop and connect it to the projector. I bring up the documents I need, as well as the most recent set of screen mock-ups. I am still finishing set-up when the architect pops in. He appears disgruntled, and I brainstorm ways to keep this meeting on track even though I know that a burning technical issue could distract us.

I decide to face the problem head-on. I ask him about the issue and whether it is urgent. He seems grateful to be acknowledged and says he wished he had thought of this potential problem earlier. It is urgent he says, but a meeting this afternoon is fine. He also needs the final documents that we are reviewing in this meeting to begin planning the next iteration's design. This is the best outcome I could have hoped for.

The product manager and two subject matter experts arrive right on time. We discuss the new project proposals being considered, the ones my manager sent to me yesterday. I get a bit of information about the second proposal that will be helpful in my estimating. At five minutes past the hour, the other developers shuffle in. We have a quorum.

Some people have printouts of the documents, but for those who don't, I bring the most recent documents up on the projector. We walk through the four-page use case, which is a step-by-step description of how the user will interact with the solution to achieve a specific goal, section by section. Collectively we ask a few questions and make some minor updates. We agree that the use case is ready for design. One more use case remains on today's agenda, and we finish our review with fifteen minutes left in the meeting.

I inquire whether everyone would like to discuss the issue that came up this morning, but we do not have a critical developer. We decide to stick with the original plan and get together this afternoon. With the remaining ten minutes, I ask a few high-level questions about the next use case on the list. I learn what is driving the feature from the product manager and about a technical constraint that the developer is concerned about. We adjourn a few minutes early.

I take a bathroom break and go back to my desk. First I see that everyone who needs to be involved in resolving the new issue is available at 3:00 p.m. I put together a brief agenda and schedule a meeting.

I note that we may only need half an hour, but I am scheduling a full hour just in case.

I open up my meeting notes template and capture my handwritten notes in electronic form. I list three new action items, or next steps that need to be taken. I add two new issues to the issues list I maintain of the open questions and concerns for the project. I also close an issue on the list and document the question's answer as the issue's resolution.

It is getting to be lunch time, so I get ready to go to the cafeteria. I used to eat lunch at my desk, but I have learned that getting away for even half an hour helps me have a more productive afternoon. Today is a beautiful day, so I throw my walking shoes in my bag as well.

I pick up my sandwich from the cafeteria line. I was planning to catch up on a few articles from a recent business analyst newsletter, but I see Bob from accounting sitting on his own. Accounting has a few process-oriented people on its team, and Bob is one of them. My ambition is to eventually establish a community of practice where everyone in our company doing business analysis tasks can share best practices, and Bob would be an influential ally. I ask if he is busy. He's not, so I sit down.

Bob and I discuss our kids' latest school project (they are both in the same school) and what sports they are considering for the summertime. We talk for a few minutes about our latest projects too. I realize that my current project could have an impact on the accounting process. Bob agrees to evaluate the requirements and determine if he can foresee any issues.

We are done with lunch. Bob waves good-bye, and I stroll outside, listening to a slice of a podcast about improving your listening skills. Most of the time I read and listen to business analysis literature, but I recently invested in a communications podcast series, and I am finding a host of new ways to improve my requirements meetings.

I get back to my desk around 12:30. I update the two use cases we reviewed this morning. I browse through my meeting notes, issues list, and use cases and then upload the updated files to the company intranet. I send an e-mail with links to all of the relevant materials to this morning's meeting invitees.

I check my calendar and see that I need to get moving on a new use case for Thursday's meeting. I spend an hour or so drafting the use case, incorporating the questions I have, and drafting a rough mock-up. Tomorrow I will give this all another review and send it out to the invitee list.

As I am working, a fellow business analyst comes back to her desk after a meeting. She is new to the team, and she is visibly frustrated. I ask her what is wrong. It turns out that the new issue on my project could impact hers as well. One of the developers brought it up in her meeting, even though the architect was not there, and it derailed her agenda. I let her know that I am scheduling some time to go over the issue later today and promise to inform her about the resolution. I also give her a few tips that I use to keep concerns like this from hindering my meetings, such as reviewing the agenda and the importance of each item at the opening of the meeting and keeping an issues list for when unexpected issues come up.

Then, I realize that I never stopped by my manager's desk, and it is already 2:30. I walk to her desk, and luckily she is there. We talk for a few minutes about the projects, and I agree to get her rough estimates and assumptions after my 3:00 p.m. meeting. She asks about the issue. I give her a brief synopsis of how it came up and how I stepped in to save everyone from a miserable e-mail chain. I tell her that I will let her know if the project is impacted substantially. She gives me an approving nod, and I go back to my desk.

I have just a few minutes to get to the 3:00 meeting. As I sit in the conference room, I review the e-mail chain one final time. I write down a few notes and decide how I am going to open the meeting. The crew wanders in and chats about the issue. I ask them to hold off on conversation until everyone is here. After all, we are here to gain consensus.

We have everyone we need, and I summarize the issue as I understand it. I ask if anyone would like to clarify what I have said, and we are off and running. Forty-five minutes and several white board drawings later, we have resolved the issue. I will need to log a small change request with the project manager. I am tired but energized. We all leave in upbeat spirits.

After a short break, I spend the remainder of my day working on the estimates for my manager. At 5:20 p.m., I finally hit send on the e-mail. Getting meeting notes out from the problem-solving session and writing up the resulting change request will have to wait until tomorrow.

No Typical Day

While the story above walks you through a probable day for a business analyst, no typical day exists. Rather, business analysts experience different kinds of days, some of which tend to repeat themselves throughout project lifecycles and some of which are unique among themselves.

Business analysis is not the type of career where you need to necessarily be prepared for anything, but expect the occasional surprise or unexpected situation. In most business analyst jobs, you will experience a fair amount of variety in your day-to-day work. And while this is not a role like technical support that requires near-constant interaction with others and real-time prioritization, priorities do shift for business analysts, and a certain amount of flexibility and responsiveness is important. Of course, if your company experiences a catastrophe or uncovers a meaningful unexpected opportunity, you may be called in to help on short notice, but that is the exception not the rule.

Most commonly your days will not hit you, instead you will hit them. The best business analysts drive the requirements process. This means scheduling meetings, managing input, influencing stakeholders, and checking that decisions are made. Excellent business analysts are proactive and seek out answers. If this is not a comfortable role for you, it might be possible to find positions where you can partner with a strong project manager. In general, however, you should be prepared for planning out your own work to meet deadlines (possibly set by yourself, possibly imposed) and facilitating input and occasionally following up with a number of people to achieve your end goals.

While no typical day exists, a business analyst can expect to experience several kinds of days.

During Project Initiation

Project initiation mainly involves eliciting requirements to understand the scope of a potential solution to a problem. Elicitation days are fun, and many business analysts enjoy elicitation days the most. These days occur early in the project or possibly even before the project commences and involve meeting with stakeholders to understand what they want to achieve in a project.

You will spend elicitation days drinking from a fire hose because you will be learning so much and handling so many different perspectives about the project. You may spend subsequent working hours typing up your copious notes and analyzing what you learned. In other environments, where the stakeholders may not be as forthcoming, you will invest more time in building trust, selling project benefits, and using many different types of elicitation techniques to obtain the information you need to help the team agree on the scope of a project.

Elicitation is an intellectual activity. All of your intellectual capabilities and strengths are stretched to the max as you help your stakeholders identify, sort, and crystallize their best ideas into concrete proposals scoping a tangible project.

After your initial interviews or facilitation sessions, you will have days where you pull together what you learned and produce readable, consumable documents identifying the scope of the project. These days may be filled with follow-up questions, e-mails, phone calls, or impromptu meetings. You will build visuals and textual documents and facilitate review sessions.

During initiation, business analysts handle ambiguity and create clarity. This phase may involve rooting out opposing opinions among stakeholders and bringing these issues to the surface. This time is full of dialogue, thinking, and communication. You draw, you write, you vet, you review. You think you have got it, only to find new flaws around the next analysis corner. You backtrack a bit, re-set, and press forward.

At times, the ambiguity might seem overwhelming. The list of open issues might be longer than the list of agreed-upon requirements. The aspects that you do not know about the current process and systems might seem more considerable than what you do know. It is not uncommon to begin to doubt whether the team will ever agree on the scope of the project and whether you as the business analyst will discover everything you need to know to safeguard a successful outcome.

What is more, if you find yourself in a new organization or working with new stakeholders or areas of the business, you will spend a fair amount of time early on getting oriented. To be successful as a business analyst, you will need to acquire basic knowledge about the system, the product, and the organization. You will also be meeting new people and learning how they work and communicate and figuring out your role on the team. You may feel like the least knowledgeable person in the room. But that is okay because it is your role to facilitate, not necessarily have all the answers.

With patience and persistence, along with some strong self-management, stakeholder management, and analysis, clarity does emerge. Once your team agrees on the essential business problem to be solved and the scope of the project, you will begin elaborating the detailed requirements that the implementation team can work from.

During Requirements Elaboration

Once you have defined the project scope, your days may take on a more syncopated pace. You will have devised and be working from a business analysis plan. Your primary work as a business analyst in this phase involves exploring specific sections of the project in more detail, by building visual models, drafting requirements documents, and reviewing them with your team. These days tend to break up into about one-third meetings and two-thirds independent work. As a new business analyst, you might be assigned to a project at this phase under the wing of a senior business analyst or project manager.

In most organizations, the bulk of time spent on projects is in elaboration. These activities bring to mind peeling the layers of an onion. You progressively delve deeper into the details and strengthen the alignment around the solution. From initiation to elaboration, a shift from ambiguity to relative certainty occurs. Not to say that elaboration is a purely logical progression. You will encounter issues, unknowns, and unexpected situations, as well as solve interesting problems. You might still feel like you are drinking from a fire hose from time to time. One need uncovers another, and so on and so forth.

As the issues become less pressing and the possibility of drastic change is minimized, you will review the requirements with the implementation team to get their input on the direction and the technical solution to the problem. Many organizations use document reviews or walk-throughs to ensure that the entire team understands the requirements and can implement them. The final requirements specifications need to blend what the business wants with what can be accomplished given project and system constraints.

During this time you will be helping negotiate trade-offs and solving technical problems. Some requirements are fairly simple to implement. Others constitute challenges and involve multiple iterations where you clarify the business need, examine the details of the possible solution, go back to the business with ideas, and iterate until you obtain consensus on a go-forward plan.

This phase is all about analyzing and facilitating groups of people to think through how to best solve problems. You will share documents for review, receive feedback, and make modifications. Repeat. Repeat. Repeat.

During Project Implementation

As developers design the system, you will be involved in discussions or formal reviews, confirming that the business requirements are fulfilled. In some organizations, formal traceability practices are in place, and you could be involved in mapping requirements to design or test documentation to make certain that the requirements are covered completely.

Once implementation begins, the business analyst (unless he or she is also filling the role of project manager) no longer drives the process, and the project may even be implemented while you get underway with a new project. You will be responding to questions from developers and testers as well as resolving issues about the requirements as they come up.

Depending on the organization's methodology, you might also be keeping documentation in sync with how the final product works. Depending on the role and other roles within the company, you may help train the business users, author help documentation, identify and implement new business processes, help to assure the quality of the delivered product, and/or facilitate user acceptance testing. But none of these activities necessarily will be the responsibility of the business analyst in a given organization.

During implementation, projects may hit snags. The business analyst might schedule an impromptu meeting to lead the team through solving a difficult problem or re-thinking a requirement. These discussions may involve identifying potential solutions to a difficult-to-address requirement or finding a work-around to an unexpected dependency within the system. It is not uncommon for discussions to become heated, especially under tight deadlines, and for the business analyst to leverage an assortment of collaboration techniques to help the team discover a suitable resolution.

But Then Again ... It's Different In An Agile Environment

All of the above is true in a traditional environment, in which projects progress from scope to detailed requirements to design to implementation to testing. In agile environments projects are broken up into short sprints in which scope, requirements, design, implementation, and testing happen within a time frame of two to four weeks. As a result of the compressed timeline, many technology roles change. Given how this trend is gaining increasing acceptance, it is likely that you will be working within an agile environment at some point in your career.

The business analyst role in agile environments is fairly ill-defined. Aspects of being the product owner, the person responsible for defining the vision and prioritizing the backlog of requirements, clearly involve business analysis activities. In an agile environment, the business analyst may either fill the product owner role or directly support the product owner.

If you find a position in an agile environment, it is safe to hypothesize that you will be doing the above sorts of activities but in shorter increments and all within the span of two to four weeks. Your days actually might be more predictable from one week to the next as you balance all of these activities to deliver just-in-time requirements.

We discuss how the business analyst role differs in different types of software development methodologies in the next chapter on business analysis skills.

Frequently Asked Questions

How Will I Be Managed?

While you will have a project manager or functional manager overseeing your work, business analysts are not customarily micromanaged. Because the role requires your best thinking and in-depth analysis, you might be the only one who really sees the whole picture of what needs to be accomplished and how you intend to get there. Even though you understand what needs to be done, expect to externalize that plan for the benefit of others who will need to be involved, as well as those, like the project managers, who will track your progress.

What Motivates A Business Analyst?

Most business analysts are self-motivated people with high standards for quality and completeness. We are motivated to discover the best possible solution to the underlying problem. Since the role is collaborative by nature, business analysts desire to improve how projects flow and how people work together. Many business analysts are also motivated by a desire to help others, whether that be by improving a frustrating system, fixing a broken process, or launching a new service that solves a real need.

Staying both focused and motivated is key to being successful as a business analyst. Given that we usually work well ahead of project delivery, it is necessary to stay on top of priorities for deadlines that are weeks if not months away. Analysis activities almost always take longer than anticipated, as unexpected issues come up. Staying ahead of the game helps safeguard a successful project.

How Will I Get Feedback About My Work?

You will receive a lot of feedback regarding your documentation, not necessarily about you personally. As a business analyst you are constantly publishing documents, visuals, and interpretations to your stakeholders and teammates for critique. Be prepared to get their honest feedback. Welcome it. This is part of the requirements process. Many business analysts are perfectionists by nature, and this can make it difficult to watch people point out your mistakes in a meeting or an e-mail. The key is to separate yourself from your deliverables. Let your deliverables take the beating. It will make them better.

Will I Be Able To Telecommute?

Business analysis is a mixed bag when it comes to telecommuting. If you plan to work locally and full-time, expect to be in the office at least three to four days per week. In-person communication is too important for this role, and struggling to communicate over the phone when you could just as easily be in the office is unnecessary. However, working one day a week from home may help you set aside time for analysis and documentation, provided that the company you work for supports this.

Even with a local office, many companies have offices across the country (and multiple countries) today, and you might be on the phone, anyway, or you might be traveling to meet with your stakeholders. In these types of corporate environments, telecommuting may be a more viable option.

What Is It Like To Work With Remote Offices?

Working with remote offices changes the role substantially. It is more difficult to build relationships and communicate over the phone and via e-mail. You need more patience and more tech savvy (to run online meetings and potentially update documents in real-time) and particularly strong communication skills.

Will I Be Required To Travel?

The amount of travel time fluctuates among business analyst positions. If you find a position with a consulting company, you could travel every week, potentially to different clients. If you find a position with a local company, you may never leave your city. But with a plethora of companies having multiple offices, it is likely that you will travel occasionally, either to conduct elicitation sessions with stakeholders in a remote office or to kick off a project with an out-sourced technology team.

In What Locations Will I Find Business Analyst Jobs?

The majority of business analyst jobs are going to be found in or near metropolitan areas, and most will be on-site. As mentioned before, the business analyst role is not particularly good for telecommuting. Consider the technology and corporate market in your area. If organizations exist that make sizeable investments in technology each year, they probably employ business analysts. If not, then you may need to consider relocating to a more tech-heavy or business-oriented market.

How Much Time Will I Spend Working With Others?

A long-time salesperson asked me if I thought a business analyst career would be suitable for him.

I asked a follow-up question (business analysts always have follow-up questions), "How much do you like working on sales proposals?"

What I wanted to know was whether this salesperson enjoyed working independently as well as talking to others.

While the amount of time a business analyst spends working with others versus working independently will vary by role and project phase, a general approximation would be to expect to spend one-third of your time interacting with others and two-thirds working independently.

It is quite possible that each individual could slightly tip the business analyst role to meet their personal balance, but if you think that you would like to spend more than 50 percent of your time interacting with others, this is probably not the career choice for you. With that much interaction with others, you simply will not have the time to perform the documentation and analysis duties that makes individuals in this role successful.

In other words, if our salesperson mostly enjoyed talking with customers and procrastinated on sales proposals or was not responsible for them at all, it is likely that business analysis would not be an excellent career choice.

At the other extreme, if you like to spend all of your time working independently and would rather not attend (let alone facilitate) meetings or be interrupted to answer questions, then you will find that most business analyst roles do not correspond to your preferred work patterns. Being a business analyst means interacting with stakeholders and collaborating with others.

What Types Of Organizations Hire Business Analysts?

In general, business analysts are hired by mid-sized to larger organizations that are growing or changing. Along with growth comes the types of changes that require business analysis: business process improvements and/or formulation of new software.

Organizations in highly regulated industries also hire business analysts. As regulations change, the company's processes and systems need to be updated accordingly.

Consulting organizations that complete projects for these types of companies also hire business analysts. Consulting organizations might serve short-term technology needs or take on enterprise-wide projects.

And while the job title of business analyst might indicate that only for-profit companies need or hire business analysts, it is not uncommon for non-profit organizations to also employ business analysts.

While all organizations can benefit from hiring business analysts, as organizations become smaller they are less inclined to hire them full-time or for long-term roles. Often business analysis responsibilities are held by someone in the organization who wears multiple hats, such as a project manager, software development manager, functional manager, or representative from a business unit.

What Types Of Projects Will I Work On?

A number of software projects may benefit from the contributions of a business analyst. Common types of projects include the following:

- Business process improvement and change
- Business intelligence/data warehousing
- New product or service development
- Customizations to existing products or services

Projects can also vary in terms of the type of solution that is implemented. Some projects focus on customizing off-the-shelf tools that are purchased. Some projects involve completely custom software development, that is they are built from scratch. Other projects involve updating existing software to solve new business problems. Still other projects do not have a technology component at all and focus solely on changes made to the business processes and functions.

Will I Ever Be Bored?

For the most part, the business analyst role is challenging and stimulating. However, no job is always exciting. Business analysis has its share of mundane activities, such as taking copious meeting notes, maintaining documents like issues logs, conducting last-pass document review meetings, finalizing the impact of seemingly trivial changes throughout a web of documentation, and at times documenting what already exists so it can be evaluated and possibly rebuilt. But the mundane details are tied to a goal, high product quality, and measured by successful teams and the lack of unforeseen complications in the eleventh hour.

Will I Make Decisions?

Business analysts tend to lead from the ground up. As a business analyst, you will not generally have direct authority over others or make the big decisions on your own, but you will have a lion's share of influence if you choose to exert it. Business analysts facilitate collaboration, research, and analyze to drive the decision-making process more frequently than they get to make the big decisions.

With Whom Will I Work?

Business analysts work with a multitude of people in different departments and different levels of the organization. You can expect to have contact with people in all sorts of positions who are not very familiar with technology and what it can do to help them. You will interview these future users and possibly even shadow them to understand how they do their jobs and help find ways that technology might solve business problems.

Even as a new business analyst, you might have some executive exposure, especially if an executive is the project sponsor or the person with budget authority and the final say on the scope of a project. You may balance executive perspectives with those of the people who work with the system day-to-day.

If you are working for a company where software is the product, you will likely have a primary contact in marketing or product management. In this scenario, your contact in product management or marketing is responsible for the vision of what is to be built, and the business analyst works with them to articulate that vision and detail the solution.

Business analysts also collaborate closely with colleagues across the technology group, primarily project managers, software developers, technology architects, and quality assurance engineers. If the project emphasizes user interface design, you might also collaborate with a user experience professional or user interface designer to maintain consistency between the design and the requirements. If the project involves organizing content, you will work with editors, content managers, corporate librarians, or other information professionals to align requirements with content organization and structure. As you move from entry-level to enterprise-level and begin to analyze the value and impact of projects and changes across the entire organization, you will also work with architects and leaders within the information technology department to scope and plan projects or align business needs with technology direction.

Will I Work More With The Business Or With The Technology Team?

It depends. If you are assigned to the project after the business owner already has a well-defined idea and your efforts are focused on working through the details, you might work with a handful of business stakeholders and then collaborate closely with the implementation team on the functional requirements. Alternatively, there might be a fair amount of exploration to be done before the idea can even crystallize. In these cases you begin further within the business by exploring the business processes and problems to be solved.

Depending upon how the role is defined within your organization, you might elaborate the project requirements to articulate every detail on every user interface screen, or your analysis work might be done when you have defined a high-level process flow and set of business requirements. Some organizations split the business analyst role into two by employing a business analyst who focuses more on the business side of the process and delivers business requirements and a systems or requirements analyst who fleshes out the business requirements into functional specifications within a system or set of systems.

How Many Hours Per Week Will I Be Expected To Work?

Business analysts normally do not work hefty amounts of over-time or work nights and weekends, though, of course, it is always possible given the company culture and project expectations. As far as career choices go, especially within technology, a full-time business analyst position with a local company will generally have fairly normal working hours. This answer is going to be different for independent consultants or individuals working as business analysts for a consulting company that requires a lot of travel.

Because the bulk of your work is in the upfront stages of a project, your activities may not be quite as deadline-driven as those responsible for the testing efforts or the implementation of the project, and overtime is usually not required. However, it is not uncommon for a business analyst to be assigned to a project where the development team is ready to begin implementing in a few short weeks, and yet there is a lot of ambiguity about the project scope and requirements. These situations involve a lot of short-term pressure to get the scope right and define the details until you can get ahead of the development team.

How Will My Work Be Defined?

In most organizations, business analysts are given a fair amount of freedom in their work and how they accomplish their objectives. In an organization with a formal software development process, the deliverables you put together may be fairly well-defined, and you may need to strictly adhere to some established templates and frameworks. There might also be formal gates that each project goes through, and a business analyst will have a critical role in bringing a project through the initial gates. In an organization with less formality or in a situation where you are the first business analyst within an organization, you might have the chance to define the requirements process.

To Whom Will I Report?

In a matrix organization you will have both a project manager to report to for project-specific deliverables and a functional manager, who will oversee the overall process and your work as a business analyst. In some organizations, the project manager is also the business analyst's supervisor.

Your functional manager may be dedicated to overseeing all or part of the business analysis group or oversee employees from multiple functional roles. For example, in my role of Enterprise Solution Director, I was responsible for the business analysis, project management, information architecture, and quality assurance roles. There were fifteen people total in this group, and we envisioned eventually establishing management roles for each department as the teams grew.

Once I Master The Basics, Will I Still Be Challenged?

Business analysts encounter one challenge after another. If you are not identifying a new business problem, you are wrestling with a new communication situation. You will need to stay abreast of technology trends and experiment with new tools and techniques. As roles blend and the options for solving complex business problems with technology expand, understanding what is available and exploring the possible applications of new technology solutions is becoming of increasing importance for business analysts.

What is not going to change all that much are the fundamentals of business analysis. If you focus on learning the fundamentals and work your way through a few projects, you will reach a point where you have mastered the basic techniques but can keep on refining the art. There is no one best way to perform business analysis work that works in every situation, so you will always be able to learn something new that might help you tomorrow, even as the underlying fundamentals remain consistent.

How Do You Measure The Success Of A Business Analyst?

While the measures of your success as a business analyst may be difficult to define, it is becoming increasingly necessary to define meaningful performance metrics that support the value that strong business analysis adds to an organization.

Successful business analysis involves a contribution to a project or other business change effort that maximizes the value realized from the solution and minimizes the effort required to implement the solution. Specifically, the business analyst helps build clarity among stakeholders, ensures that the problem is well understood, and makes certain that the solution is clear and complete.

Measurements related to business analysis work may be considered at the project level and at the level of the business analysis effort itself.

At the project level, you might consider how the business analyst contributes to the following project-success measures:

- On-time delivery
- On-budget delivery
- On-specification delivery
- Return on investment (ROI)

At the level of the business analyst effort, you might consider measurements such as:

- Minimized requirements changes requested late in the project
- Minimized requirements defects discovered after approval
- Efficiency of the requirements effort
- Increased business benefits (the return part of ROI)

Adriana Beal covers this topic in depth and identifies many common measurement pitfalls in her e-book entitled *Measuring the Performance of Business Analysts.*

How Difficult Will It Be To Find A Job?

If you are truly passionate about being a business analyst and most of the responsibilities required come naturally to you, it should not be any more difficult to find a business analyst position than it is to find a job in most other professions. In some respects, the barriers to entry are lower than other information technology jobs because no expectations for formal training or specific technical knowledge exist. The technical skills of a business analyst are relatively easy to learn but might take a lifetime to perfect. No one stamp of approval makes you a business analyst, so you might spend some time gathering relevant experiences and learning the techniques.

On the other hand, many business analyst positions require individuals with experience. Because no single path into the profession works for everyone and no degree will qualify you for a position, it may be challenging to carve a path into your first position. Devising situations where you can get the necessary experiences or finding someone who recognizes your talents in lieu of your experience is the challenge.

On a related note, business analysis skills will remain relatively timeless. While software development skills become quickly outdated, business analysis is not changing quite so fast. This makes it an advantageous profession for people experimenting with multiple careers or leaving the professional world for a period of time to raise children or pursue other interests.

What Impact Will I Have?

Just like most professions, business analysts may work in non-profit and other worthy organizations, but as a profession, business analysis is not geared toward noble work. Your requirements could have an adverse impact on society or a positive one. It really depends on the vision of your stakeholder. Of course, as an independent professional, you choose who you work for and what kind of work you do.

The impact a business analyst makes is most keenly felt within the organization or by its customers. As a representative of the organization's diverse set of individuals who use software every day to accomplish their objectives, your mission to make the software better can help make these individuals' work days more productive and efficient. The software may automate repetitive tasks and allow individuals to focus on more complex tasks. Or, quite honestly, the software you help design could put people out of a job.

Sometimes business analysts are being brought into organizations where the role did not exist before. In these situations, you may make an impact on the work lives of the technical team. Recent studies suggest that poor requirements practices account for many project failures. Set cost savings aside, and consider the lives of individuals on these teams as they work day-by-day on a project headed toward failure, struggling to write code for unclear or non-existent requirements, participating in heated discussions with no resolution, and time spent working on features that never see the light of day. Business analysts insert themselves into the thick of these situations and may have a positive impact on the relationships between project team members. This is part of what personally keeps me going when I am working through some of the more mundane details involved with being a business analyst.

Putting It To Practice #2

List The Pros And Cons

First, let's talk about the pros. Consider the above details about the role of business analyst, and list a few that energized you. Write a few sentences, or paragraphs if you are inspired, about what that experience means to you. What made you excited about becoming a business analyst? How will you feel doing these activities? What will be fun? What more do you want to know about this part of the job?

Next, let's consider the cons. Now go back through the items that made you ponder or possibly even doubt your decision. Write as precisely as you can why these aspects of the job made you nervous. Do you feel that you would dislike something about that task? Are you unsure if you could do it?

Clarifying your uncertainties can help transform indecision into confidence. Do not let your doubts become barriers. Instead, focus on what you can do to learn a bit more about this area of business analysis. For example, some of our course participants take a class just to experiment with a new business analyst skill and see if it comes easily to them.

You will not have to go through this process alone, as we will walk through exactly how to get answers to your questions and doubts in later chapters. For now, after you have explored the above questions, make a list of additional questions in your notebook.

✓ Putting It To Practice #3

Evaluate Business Analyst Job Descriptions

As you are considering entering a new profession, one of the most beneficial things you can do is to develop habits that promote ongoing learning. One habit I have found particularly constructive is to stay aware of the language used in job postings. Spend some time each week reviewing the business analyst postings on a number of job boards. Print or save the ones that seem the most relevant to you or have a unique aspect that interests you.

As you develop this habit, go beyond business analyst positions to other related positions that require business analysis skills. As you incorporate this habit of learning into your weekly routine, you will be amazed at how your awareness of positions, jobs, and roles increases.

CHAPTER
2

What You Need To Know About Business Analysis

Always act from a position of strength.
~ Woody Pastorius (one of my most influential mentors)

As you consider your business analysis career ambitions, one important factor to note is the skills and competencies you bring to the table, as well as the skills and competencies you need to develop to be successful. In this chapter, we will look at the key skills required to be successful in all types of business analyst roles.

But first I am going to share a funny story with you.

One evening, I ran down the short flight of stairs in our home after putting our daughter to bed. I smiled at my husband, who had an odd expression on his face. I stared at him to figure out why.

I walked over to where he sat and said, "What's that goofy face for?"

He said, "You didn't see them, did you?"

Puzzled, I responded, "See what?"

He shifted his eyes back toward the stairs. On the ledge in front of our stairway were a dozen yellow roses, in plain sight.

I could not believe that I had completely missed them. For a split second, I even thought that maybe my husband had teleported them there, but then I remembered the laws of physics and found my own eyes to be the culprit.

I was studying my husband and his funny expression instead of what was right in front of me.

This same sort of thing happens to all of us, all of the time. We do not see what may be obvious to other people or even what other people expect that we should be seeing. In all the work I do with professionals aspiring to get ahead in the business analysis profession, the most prevalent problem I see is that they fail to notice relevant and transferable skills from their own career background. As a result, they perceive themselves to be less qualified to do business analysis than they truly are.

My hope is that this chapter will help you see the bouquet of roses waiting for you on the ledge at the bottom of the stairs. If you have even a few years of professional experience, quite plausibly you have business analysis skills and competencies that you can draw from. Discovering your transferable skills and experiences is an investment, but it will yield dividends by accelerating your journey into business analysis.

To make the most of this chapter, read it through one time to take in the content, and then read it a second time and categorize your level of strength for each skill. It is possible for you to understand a skill even if you have never held the business analyst job title or you have used a different term to refer to the work you did. So think broadly here, and when unsure, give yourself the benefit of the doubt.

We will start by evaluating the underlying core competencies required to be a business analyst and then look at skills specific to the business analysis profession. Finally we will consider some broader knowledge areas that business analysts need to know about, including software development methodologies, tools, and domain-specific skills.

This chapter focuses on the competencies and skills required to perform business analysis for a project, as that is where we see the bulk of business analysis jobs in the marketplace today.

Underlying Core Competencies

Underlying business analysis core competencies are the qualities relevant to business analysis but that are not specific to the profession. If business analysis is a suitable career choice, you will have experience applying many of the underlying core competencies in other professional capacities.

In this section, we will specifically bear in mind how business analysts benefit from utilizing these underlying core competencies. As you consider each skill, keep in mind that you may be able to present evidence of the competency in a capacity not directly related to business analysis.

Problem-Solving And Critical Thinking

No project is without problems. In fact, projects are a solution to a problem. Business analysts facilitate a shared understanding of the problem, the possible solutions, and determine the scope of the project. Like we saw in our sample work day, you will also find business analysts in the midst of facilitating teams to solve technical challenges, especially when they involve negotiation between multiple business or technical stakeholders.

When it comes to problems, business analysts are responsible for evaluating multiple options before helping a team settle on a solution. While discovering the problem to be solved, business analysts must listen to stakeholder needs but also critically consider those needs and ask probing questions until the real need surfaces and is understood. This is what makes critical thinking and evaluation skills important for new business analysts.

Below are some indications that problem-solving and critical thinking are strengths for you:

- When using a new product, service, or website, do you tend to see how it can be improved?

- When using a new product, service, or website, do you think about how the process works internally as well as from your perspective as a customer? Alternatively, do you think about how your organization's products, services, or website works from the perspective of those outside the organization?
- Can you recall experiences where you collaborated with multiple people to resolve an issue?
- Can you recall experiences where you helped determine that the original stated issue was different than the actual root cause of the issue?
- Even when a sound solution presents itself, do you tend to explore other options just in case a better solution emerges?

Analytical Thinking

One of the most fundamental skills business analysts must possess is the ability to analyze. A business analyst analyzes the input of stakeholders with the goal of creating a comprehensive understanding of the change to be made. Analysis is the process of solving the actual problem, in terms of specifying requirements, producing visuals that represent the new process or software application, and developing workflows and business processes.

Many business analysts focus on the documentation aspect of the role, which we will look at in more detail under the Business Analysis Skills section. It is important to realize that requirements specifications are the result of detailed analysis about a set of requirements. Some types of specifications do heavily support the analysis process by encouraging thinking about flows, rules, exceptions, and boundaries. For example, a use case is one type of requirements specification. A use case contains a section for exceptions, which encourages the business analyst to think about what could go wrong within a specific flow of events and specify how the system should respond to those errors.

In breaking down the problem, the business analyst finds inconsistencies between what the stakeholders want and what makes logical sense. Throughout the analysis process, the business analyst brings stakeholders from multiple business and technology departments together to work through how to solve a specific problem, given project or system constraints.

Below are some signs that analytical thinking is a strength for you:

- After discussing a problem and a solution, do you tend to have more questions that need to be answered or think of implications that others miss?
- When a group of people is discussing solutions to a problem, do you tend to find common threads in their ideas?
- Can you recall experiences when you solved a business or technical problem completely?

Relationship-Building

We cannot always directly control our success in business analysis, rather we depend upon the input, participation, and knowledge of others to fashion a successful outcome. Business analysts include others and generate more successful outcomes by forging strong relationships with stakeholders, managers, sponsors, implementers, and team members.

The importance of relationships was demonstrated in nearly every hour of our sample work day. Our business analyst chose to eat lunch with Bob from accounting instead of eating alone. By doing so, she invested in the relationship and inched forward a long-term career goal of implementing a community of practice. She also was able to secure his input even though he was not formally assigned to her project team.

A second example was more subtle. Before her requirements meeting got underway, a stakeholder offered her information about a pending project that would help her with her estimate. Do you think this information would have been offered to an unknown or untrusted person?

Additional examples included how our business analyst addressed the newly-surfaced issue with the architect and how she addressed the frustrations of her teammate. Through her interactions with others and the way she chose to step into leadership roles, our business analyst showed her skill in building relationships and earning trust.

Below are some indications that relationship-building is a strength for you:

- Do you make a point to visit with your co-workers outside of a formal meeting setting?
- Do your co-workers come to you for help with their work-related problems and concerns?
- Do you have a network of people inside and outside your organization that you can ask for help when you face a new challenge?
- Do people trust you with sensitive information? Do you honor their trust?
- Are you able to get things done through collaboration? Do you encourage others to pitch in on your projects?

Self-Management

While business analysts are not project managers, the most successful business analysts manage the business analysis effort. This means that the business analyst is proactive and dependency-aware. It also means that they manage themselves to commitments and deadlines, a skill set which may involve influence, delegation, and issue management.

In our sample day, our business analyst was responsible for meeting deadlines. We saw our business analyst plan ahead to complete deliverables needed a few days out and be aware of how an urgent issue could impact the overall project timeline. She also managed an issues list to keep on top of important concerns and delegate research tasks across the project team.

Below are some signs that self-management is an area of strength for you:

- Do you plan the work that you will accomplish in a given day? In a given week?
- Are you able to plan ahead to deadlines a month or more out and make a timeline for achieving them?
- When issues surface that could impact your timeline for a project, are you able to implement contingency plans to minimize the impact?
- Do you rarely find yourself surprised at the eleventh hour by work that must be done by others before you can finish a task?
- Do you consciously update others about your work, such as your manager, project manager, and other stakeholders?

A Thick Skin

Business analysts receive a barrage of feedback about their documentation and proposed solutions. They also deal with sensitive issues and may find themselves in the midst of tension and disagreement. To succeed as a business analyst you need to be able to separate feedback about your documents and ideas from feedback about you personally.

While the business analyst in our sample work day at first hesitated to bring up the touchy issue with the architect, she was able to get past her initial fear of the architect's reaction. As a result, the short conversation directly impacted the effectiveness of her meeting. Of course, her approach could have backfired, and the architect could have given the business analyst some negative feedback or decided to go on and on about the issue. The business analyst put the quality of the meeting ahead of her own ego and asked the question. This is an example of having a thick skin.

Below are some indications that you have a thick skin:

- When someone points out a mistake you made, do you seek to find the root cause and resolve it promptly? (Alternatively, if your skin needs thickening, you might spend more time worrying about the mistake and less time fixing it.)
- When a document you created is reviewed by others, do you hope for feedback so that you can make it better? (Alternatively, if your skin needs thickening, you might await feedback anxiously and second-guess every one of your reviewers.)
- Can you recall an experience when your idea was rejected and you willingly went along with the new idea because you agreed that it was better?

Even if you do not currently have a thick skin, it can be cultivated over time. Being aware of your sensitivities and how they might impact your business analysis work is the first step toward working past them so that you can accept feedback more openly, objectively, and graciously.

Driving Improvements

While business analysts are not usually decision-makers, they still fill critical leadership roles on projects. Business analysts drive change, overcome resistance, and keep projects moving forward.

The business analyst must keep the goal of the project in perspective and align their efforts as well as the efforts of the project's stakeholders toward that goal. Business analysts are regularly in the unique position to see positive outcomes and help project sponsors and other stakeholders buy into the possibilities enabled by change. Throughout the entire business analysis process, the analyst must also keep the project moving forward, unfailingly transforming ambiguity into clarity.

As a business analyst, you may find yourself facing resistance to change from one or more stakeholder groups on your project. Resistance can be passive, such as a stakeholder withholding critical information that is needed to identify the requirements for a project. Resistance can also be active, such as a stakeholder moving forward with a different approach than the one that the team has agreed to. A strong business analyst is aware of all kinds of resistance and uses a number of techniques to bring all of the project stakeholders into alignment.

Business analysts also anticipate resistance and take proactive actions to effect buy-in early in their projects. I once worked with a project manager who had tremendous skills in this area. The executive leadership had decided to build a new online portal for use by their customers. In another office, there were stakeholders from four different departments that interacted with these customers. The executives did not directly involve the directors of these departments in their decision to fund the project. Moreover, there was a history of these stakeholders directly and indirectly resisting technology and process changes.

The project manager's first step was to meet with these stakeholders and describe the executive vision. She took care to frame the vision in such a way that emphasized the benefits to members of the four teams. Then she shifted the discussion and sought to understand the stakeholders' frustrations with the current processes. Finally, she suggested many adjustments to the scope of the project so that the stakeholders' frustrations were addressed while still fulfilling key elements of the executive vision. As a result, we experienced unprecedented buy-in and engagement from these four departments, and the project proceeded rather smoothly.

Below are some signs that driving improvements is a strength for you:

- Can you see a future that's better than what exists today? Can you effectively describe a future that does not yet exist to others?
- Do you help others see the benefits of embracing change?
- Do you actively seek to understand why others might resist change and take proactive steps to confirm their buy-in?
- Do you find ways to keep your projects moving forward?
- Do your projects and efforts tend to fulfill your sponsor's original vision and goals?

Communicating

Business analysts must be powerful communicators. This means that they can facilitate working meetings, ask insightful questions, listen to the answers (really listen), and absorb what is being said. In today's world, communication does not always happen face-to-face. The ability to be a strong communicator in a virtual setting, such as through conference calls or web meetings, is equally important.

Communication takes many forms for the business analyst, and you will see threads relating back to communication come up in many of the skills more specific to business analysis that are listed below. A business analyst communicates about the requirements, about the design, and about the issues. You help others communicate amongst themselves to agree about a problem or a solution. You communicate verbally, in pictures, and in written documentation.

While it may seem counter-intuitive, one of the most important verbal communication skills you can develop is your ability to actively listen. Listening involves the act of hearing at a most basic level but is really about understanding and asking relevant questions until you develop a shared understanding with the person speaking. Being a careful listener and asking perceptive questions are two trademark skills for a business analyst. Regardless of your current profession and employment status, you have occasions to use and improve on these skills every day.

Below are some indications that you are a strong communicator:

- Do you have experience facilitating or speaking up in meetings, both virtual and face-to-face?
- Do you commonly hear what others do not and ask questions to clarify what is being said?
- Are you able to translate between groups that use different terminology to talk about the same topics?
- Do your e-mails and documents generally get read, and do you have evidence that they are understood as you intended them to be?
- Do you use alternate ways to communicate information, such as pictures, charts, and other types of visual representations?

In this section, we have looked at the underlying core competencies held by business analysts. Your experience applying these skills in other roles and environments will serve you well as you launch your business analyst career. Now, let's turn our attention to skills that are more specific to the business analysis profession.

Business Analysis Skills

Like any profession or industry, business analysts use a lot of jargon to talk about what they do and how they do it. It is easy for the jargon to trip up new business analysts. One attendee of a complimentary webinar I gave told a story of being asked about his experience with prototypes in a job interview. He told his interviewer that he did not have any relevant experience. Upon discussing prototypes in our session, he learned that his experience producing what he called wireframes was relevant and could have secured him the position. (If both prototypes and wireframes are unfamiliar to you, do not worry, they are addressed below.)

Another course participant had recently interviewed for a job and was asked about his experience with use cases. Similarly, he said he did not have any experience. Upon taking our course on use cases, he learned that he had documented a similar type of requirements in a different format. Again, he could have made the connection but did not. Six months later this same person was hired to help an organization adopt more formal requirements methodologies, and one of his responsibilities would be to teach others in his organization to analyze requirements in use cases.

These stories tell us that knowing the business analysis language is important. In this section, we will discuss some of the more frequently used business analysis terms that come up as job requirements so you know what they mean and are able to identify your relevant skill sets.

Collaboration Techniques

As a business analyst, you will collaborate with stakeholders from all areas of the business and technology teams. The work experiences you have participating in collaborative efforts will be relevant to a future business analyst role. Business analysts use many specific techniques to collaborate with stakeholders, and these fall primarily in the areas of elicitation and validation.

Let's talk a bit more about each of these in turn.

Elicitation is the process of working with stakeholders to understand what they want to achieve through the project or change effort. A business stakeholder is anyone who has an interest in the change or influence over the change. Stakeholders might have a clear picture of what they want, or they might be vague and use ambiguous language. Some stakeholders are clear about the vision but fuzzy on the details. Others think clearly about the details but lose track of the big picture. Elicitation involves bringing out the best thoughts and ideas about the change from all stakeholders.

Although elicitation will be one of the first business analysis activities on a project, it does not end with the initial requirements elicitation activities. You will come back to elicitation throughout the requirements lifecycle as you help the team achieve a clearer picture of what the change entails.

Like elicitation, validation also requires a lot of collaboration with stakeholders. Requirements validation involves ensuring that the requirements are ready for implementation or that an implemented solution solves the business problem.

Validation takes countless different forms. In formal organizations where the requirements specifications are viewed as contracts, validation involves the business stakeholders formally signing off on the requirements and the implementation team formally accepting them as buildable. In less formal organizations, validation is part of the natural flow of reviewing deliverables and handing them off for implementation.

Although validation is regularly thought of in the context of traditional software development methods, a team deploying agile practices, where development work is broken up into short sprints, also validates requirements. Validation may happen as part of a sprint planning session, the collaborative meeting taking place at the beginning of each sprint to review the requirements slated for development and plan its implementation or as part of demonstrating working software at the end of the sprint.

With the context of elicitation and validation in mind, let's look next at the most common collaboration techniques used by business analysts.

Interviews

By far the most common collaboration technique used by business analysts is the interview, whether a one-on-one interview or in a group interview session. Because interviews are a common technique to address many different business problems, you have probably conducted an interview somewhere in your previous work.

Interviews involve thoughtful questioning and active listening. As a business analyst, you want to internalize as much of what others have to say as possible. During elicitation it is less important that you fully analyze what you hear than that you actually comprehend it, have the tools in place to remember the salient points (perhaps by taking notes), and can follow up with the analysis at a later time.

Key skills for elicitation interviews include:

- **Organizing meetings** ~ Effective elicitation sessions are well-coordinated, which involves inviting the right people, setting a meeting goal, crafting an agenda, and documenting meeting notes.

- **Facilitating discussions** ~ In order to discover the information you need to move the project forward, you will need to initiate topics of discussion, keep the dialogue moving, and maintain focus on the topic at hand. The best meeting facilitators keep track of the discussion, elicit input from everyone, re-direct conversation around overly forceful personalities or off-topic comments, and drive follow-up on open points in the discussion.
- **Asking questions** ~ At the heart of any elicitation agenda are questions to be asked and answered. The business analyst asks insightful questions that drive to a deeper understanding of the problem or the solution.
- **Clarifying terminology** ~ Many disagreements about requirements and rules have their root in terminology confusion. Skilled business analysts learn to clarify terms to gain agreement about fundamental concepts.
- **Relationship-building** ~ Elicitation requires trust, and foundational to trust is building relationships with your stakeholders. They need to trust that you are on their side and will do what you can to help them see their ideas through to fruition.

Observation

Sometimes our stakeholders have difficulty answering our questions or telling us what they want. In these situations, business analysts might turn to the observation technique. As the term would suggest, observation is the process of observing a stakeholder perform their work. It is used to understand the current state of the business process and helps the business analyst discover problems to be addressed within a feature or the scope of a project.

While a pure application of the observation technique would require the business analyst to be a silent observer of the stakeholder at work in their native environment, more often observation involves dialogue. In the most common application of the observation technique, the stakeholder performs selected tasks while talking the business analyst through those tasks. The business analyst asks follow-up questions to clarify the details of the business process. This type of observation could occur in the stakeholder's native environment, in a conference room, or using desktop-sharing technology. For business processes that involve multiple stakeholders, a group walk-through may be used to identify how the hand-offs between different stakeholders and departments occur.

Structured Walk-Through

Structured walk-throughs may be used when the requirements document needs to be approved or baselined before implementation can begin. They are intended to confirm that all stakeholders have a common understanding of the project scope and detailed requirements. The reality of our busy office lives is that people are much more apt to absorb the content of a document when a walk-through takes place and they hear comments from others than when they review a document independently.

A structured walk-through involves stepping through a requirements specification or a visual model section-by-section while encouraging questions and comments. The discussion that occurs during a structured walk-through may result in unexpected issues surfacing, new requirements being identified, and ambiguities in the documented requirements being clarified. One comment tends to generate another, and everyone benefits from the critical thinking of others in the room. These meetings are frequently collaborative, as stakeholders across the project team work to understand the requirements and the solution.

A close companion to the structured walk-through is the demo, which uses a similar set of processes to review a technology solution. Let's explore how demos work.

Demo

A demo involves showing working software to project stakeholders and subject matter experts to validate that what is built meets their needs. Demos are powerful because when people see how the new process or software will work, they frequently provide new requirements and important clarifications. Demos elicit what are called *yes-but* responses that are extremely helpful in determining missing requirements.

For example, upon reviewing a new screen that will be used to add a new customer to the database, a stakeholder might say, "*yes,* this form asks for all the required information, *but* don't we need the first name and last name to be two separate fields?"

Demos can also be conducted before effort is invested in building working software. An analyst can mock up sample screens using a wire-framing tool and then walk stakeholders through the look and feel, navigation, and layout of the screens. Demos of wireframes produce valuable feedback early in the requirements process and are especially useful in minimizing requirements changes downstream.

Demos are also useful when the solution involves selecting one of several available software packages or services. Demos can be used to compare solutions, and the organization might choose to pilot one or more solutions before making a final selection.

User Acceptance Testing

User acceptance testing (UAT) involves having the intended users of the system use the working software in a demo environment to validate if it meets their needs and supports their business processes. Unlike a demo, in which the business analyst uses the software to show a pre-defined path, UAT enables business stakeholders to use the system themselves.

UAT is structured around specific business process scenarios that form the business-facing test cases. UAT goes beyond functional testing, which is focused on the observable behavior of the software, in that it tests the software in conjunction with the business processes. During UAT, business users flesh out any missing requirements or previously unnoticed business process changes and training needs before the solution is deployed.

UAT can be led by a quality assurance engineer, a business analyst, a project manager, or a primary stakeholder within the organization. As a business analyst, you might be asked to provide input in terms of the business process scenarios. You might also be involved in vetting the new requirements that surface during UAT.

Requirements Specifications

Requirements specifications are the primary deliverables produced by a business analyst. Requirements specifications are used to document and confirm the requirements related to a project or change and serve as a central communication tool about the requirements within a project. Skilled business analysts write clear, unambiguous requirements and organize them in usable documents that are well organized and easy for stakeholders to review and comment on.

As a new business analyst, you will want to be familiar with what each of the following deliverables is and knowledgeable about how you would go about producing it. You will also want to be able to speak to why you might choose a specific deliverable and what value each deliverable adds to the requirements process. Entire books are available on most types of specifications. This section provides a cursory guide and checklist to encourage you to reflect on the experience and skills you may already have or may need to develop further.

The Difference Between Requirements And Technical Design Details

Before we examine the different types of specifications, let's discuss one of the most common requirements-related debates you will find in technology circles, and that is whether a certain expression about a project is a requirement or an aspect of the technical design. The most basic answer is that requirements express what is wanted while technical design details how to build what is wanted. But as you write requirements, you will discover many expressions that fall in gray areas.

As a new business analyst, it will be easy to fall into traps of allowing business users to tell you how they want the system to be built instead of what it needs to do. Being persistent in asking why and clarifying business problems can help uncover many hidden requirements, keeping the requirements specifications focused on what is actually wanted.

Scope Statements

Scope statements result from the initial elicitation activities and define the scope of and the justification for a change from the business perspective. A scope statement typically includes a list of high-level features or business requirements to be included in the project. The features or business requirements are not captured in adequate detail to be implementable, but they are concrete and drive the activities of a project. You can think of scope statements as a roadmap for a project or initiative, clearly defining boundaries around what is to be achieved, what business objective will be fulfilled, and what is not in scope.

Functional Requirements

A functional requirements document or list details the intended functions of a new software or system. Most often, functional requirements start with *The system shall* or *The ability to* and are grouped logically by feature. For a multi-month project, a functional requirements document might easily be in excess of fifty pages. These types of documents best support projects using a version of the waterfall methodology.

Functional requirements are customarily given attributes to classify them or group them together in meaningful ways. Some common attributes are:

- Priority
- Owner
- Requestor
- Effort
- Risk

Use Cases

Use cases provide an alternative way to capture functional requirements. Use cases are textual descriptions of an interaction between one or more actors and one or more systems. They can be accompanied by use case diagrams or system interaction diagrams that visually depict the flow between the actor(s) and the system(s).

Use cases can be written at varying levels of granularity, from a high-level business process describing the flow through multiple systems to a low-level interaction between two systems or the steps to accomplish a specific business task within a single system.

By and large, use cases are one of the most fundamental techniques of business analysis. *Writing Effective Use Cases*, by Alistair Cockburn, is a time-tested resource on this topic.

Product Backlog

The product backlog is a rank-ordered list of features or requirements used to plan development activities in an agile environment.

Backlog items are ordinarily expressed in the following way: *As a [user], I want to [do something] to [achieve some objective].*

The individual items on a product backlog might be at different levels of detail, and a distinction is made between epics and stories. Epics are high-level descriptions of functionality that might encompass a few weeks to a few months of development effort, analogous to a feature or a business requirement. Stories tend to be small enough to be achieved in a few days, analogous to a functional requirement. Like functional requirements, product backlog items might also have attributes.

User Stories And Acceptance Tests

User stories are the details behind the product backlog items and how requirements are defined in an agile environment, normally via a set of acceptance tests. Once the tests pass, the story is considered complete. Some teams document user stories on physical index cards that get torn up once they are obsolete or complete. Others use electronic databases to store this information.

User Stories Applied by Mike Cohn provides a summary of what user stories are and how they function as requirements for delivery software in an agile environment.

User Interface Specifications

User interface specifications detail the rules for a specific screen or page within a system. They help you analyze the rules behind a screen and ensure that all the required functionality has a home within the new system. A user interface specification may or may not be a business analysis task, as this may be considered an element of design and not requirements. However, user interface specifications may be tremendously helpful in sorting out potential requirements issues and the communicating of requirements where the workflow of the application and the look and feel are important to the business stakeholders.

Traceability Matrices

Part of the analysis process is to check that every business requirement is fulfilled by one or more functional requirements and that every functional requirement links back to a business requirement. As you move deeper into the details about a project, a traceability matrix helps keep requirements at different levels organized. Some organizations also trace requirements to elements of the design or test cases that validate that the requirement was implemented correctly.

Diagrams And Visual Models

Equally important as textual requirements specifications is the ability to express ideas, concepts, and solutions in a visual way. Business analysts use diagrams to visually depict process flows, relationships between concepts, or to model systems or project scope.

Visual communication can be formal, such as a UML (Unified Modeling Language) diagram or other standard modeling notation. It may also be informal, such as drawing on a white board. Many middle-ground areas exist, such as basic flow charts that appear more formal in that they use some notation but are much less involved than a modeling language such as UML.

When thinking of diagrams and visual models, new business analysts characteristically turn to formal models built using sophisticated modeling toolsets, a few of which will be discussed below in the Tools section. However, informal visual modeling frequently happens during collaborative discussions as well.

One particularly vibrant memory for me related to visual modeling goes way back to my first big project as a business analyst. We were building a new e-book platform and needed to figure out how to get three different internally-developed technology systems to talk to one another. After many discussions and debates over the requirements, we finally pulled the development leads and business owners for each system into a room and discussed our options.

Ideas ping-ponged back and forth, each shot down in turn. As some options emerged, I drew on the white board. Each person contributed a piece of the idea, and I added to the drawing. Soon there were lines crossing over each other. Boxes got wiped away only to be drawn again. At the end of the conversation we had a working model of the integrated system design that conveyed how information would be passed back and forth. I brought in my laptop and captured the model in Microsoft® Visio.

Many visual models originate and end as informal white board drawings or chicken scratch on paper. As you consider your skills in diagrams and visual models, think about any experience you have both in creating formal models and in producing similar models in less formal ways.

Workflow Diagrams

Workflow diagrams, also called process flow diagrams, are an intuitive way for stakeholders to understand the organization's fundamental processes, get clarity about how work gets done, and appreciate how value is delivered. They also put other requirements activities in context. For example, a business process diagram can help facilitate more effective use case reviews by providing context for how the system functionality will support the business process.

Workflow diagrams exist in multiple forms. Most business analysts put together workflow diagrams that show the end-to-end business process. In their simplest and most common form, workflow diagrams include a box for each activity or step in the process and arrows connecting the boxes to show the sequence of steps. Diamonds can also be used to represent decisions or alternatives through the sequence of steps.

Wireframes/Mock-Ups/Prototypes

Wireframes, mock-ups, and prototypes are terms used to refer to a collection of documentation or functional code that is used to express the look and feel or page layout of an application or website. The terms wireframes and mock-ups are commonly used to refer to lower fidelity and static representations of the user interface while the term prototype is used to refer to a higher fidelity and functional representation.

Wireframes and mock-ups can be drawn on a white board or using a range of wire-framing tools (see below). Prototypes might be constructed of skeletal programming code or built using a simulation tool.

Site Map Or Screen Diagram

A site map labels, organizes, and defines the pages of a website. A site map is especially helpful for a web-based application. A correlating deliverable for an installable software application is a screen diagram. If you are building new screens or pages, or changing existing screens or pages, a map can help you lay out the scope of the application early on and identify gaps in your solution.

Data Modeling Specifications

Data models, data matrices, and data mapping specifications communicate requirements in projects where new information storage structures are being developed or when data is pushed or pulled between systems. Data models are considered closer to design than requirements, but they still may fall into the business analyst's realm of responsibility.

One of the more common types of data models is an Entity Relationship Diagram (ERD). An ERD models entities, relationships between entities, and attributes of each entity.

ERDs can be used to represent data models at different levels of abstraction. A business-level domain model describes key business concepts. A logical data model describes the specific data fields to be stored by an information storage system. A physical data model describes the actual fields and tables.

More detailed data models or data matrices include information about each attribute, such as the data type, allowable values, and whether each attribute is required or optional. A data matrix is usually captured in table form using a spreadsheet.

A data mapping specification shows how data is transferred from one information repository to another. A data mapping specification includes rules for default values, translation rules, allowable values, and optional versus required values.

A Note About UML And BPMN

Unified Modeling Language (UML) is a specific modeling language used to express the requirements and design of software systems. Several types of UML diagrams exist. Those most frequently delivered by business analysts include domain diagrams, use case diagrams, activity diagrams, and sequence diagrams.

A BPMN (Business Process Modeling and Notation) is another formal modeling notation. Business analysts use BPMN to portray more formalized business process diagrams instead of drawing simple workflow diagrams. BPMN includes many more notation options and may be used to depict more sophisticated representations of a business process in such a way that it can be automated and managed.

Neither UML nor BPMN are common job requirements, and the necessity for these skills will be highly dependent on the business analysis process in place at a given organization. Generally, UML and BPMN are skills to pick up once you have some business analysis experience.

Related Skills

Like any profession, the core skill set and underlying competencies only tells part of the story. Additional skills also play a role in qualifying one for specific business analyst jobs. In this section, we evaluate the software development methodologies and toolsets you will want to be familiar with as a business analyst and then consider the domain-specific skills that are part of many business analyst job postings.

Software Development Methodologies

Software development cycles characterize how an organization approaches a project. As a business analyst, you will likely work with an array of methodologies and software development cycles. An awareness of software development lifecycles will help you anticipate how your deliverables fit into the overall flow of project work. You will want to know what the different methodologies are, stay aware of current literature on new and existing methodologies, and most importantly, understand the adaptations of the business analyst role within each methodology.

Waterfall

Hardly any organization will admit that it is using waterfall anymore, and this methodology is the butt of many jokes and passionate criticisms. The reality, however, is that many organizations use some modification of the waterfall process.

A waterfall methodology is exactly what it sounds like: each phase of the project (requirements, design, development, test, and implementation) occurs in linear order and concludes with a big splash at the end for delivery. While decidedly out of vogue, it can still be useful in small projects.

More importantly, you should understand why waterfall is out of vogue and the issues caused by a large, upfront requirements process un-vetted by design and implementation. A core argument against a waterfall methodology is that stakeholders provide the best possible feedback when presented with working software. By saving working software to the end of the process, a solution implemented using a waterfall methodology may fail to meet stakeholder expectations.

A second argument against waterfall is based on the reality that today's organizations change and evolve rapidly. Since waterfall methodologies support a lock-down of requirements early in a project, routinely as much as six to twelve months or more before delivering working software, they inhibit the organization from effectively responding to change.

Many organizations' methodologies use more of the waterfall process than they would like to admit, even when they use different terms to talk about their process, so it is important to understand how to recognize a waterfall process when you see one.

Iterative

Iterative software development methodologies address many of the problems with the waterfall process by breaking a sizable project down into iterations. With each iteration of delivery, a set of requirements go from design to development to testing in a shorter duration of time to allow for feedback loops.

The most common iterative process is the Rational Unified Process (RUP). The essential principals of the RUP include attacking major risks early, maintaining a focus on quality throughout the project, and maintaining a focus on value. RUP focuses on creating an executable architecture early in the project lifecycle so subsequent project iterations can be built in interlocking sub-components.[4]

In the RUP, after an initial collaborative phase to define the scope of the project and define the architectural plan, detailed requirements are tackled in iterations and typically documented as use cases. This technique helps maintain a focus on value to the individual business stakeholders for each piece of functionality.

In an iterative process, the business analyst is involved heavily up front, identifying the vision and key business objectives. The business analyst is also involved throughout the project lifecycle, breaking the key features into iterations and collaborating with the business and technology teams around the detailed requirements.

The RUP is sometimes managed through IBM's Rational® tools. Organizations employing a formal version of the RUP methodology may have also invested in the Rational® Toolset, and experience with Rational's RequisitePro™, Clear Case™, and/or ClearQuest™ might be necessary. Prior to agile, RUP was the best-in-class iterative process. RUP still provides the foundational thinking behind many agile processes.

Agile

For the last several years, agile methodologies have been making the transition from the latest fad in software development to an emerging, respectable trend in the business community. At their core, agile methodologies favor short, incremental development to get working software in front of users as early as possible. Agile methodologies focus on collaboration, interaction, and responding to change over processes, documentation, and following a plan.

---

[4] *The Rational Unified Process Made Easy.* Kroll and Krutchen. Page 5.

To learn more about agile methodologies, read the Agile Manifesto[5], a short, fundamental text outlining the principles of agile software development, available for free online. Consider reading *Scaling Software Agility: Best Practices for Large Enterprises* by Dean Leffingwell for a thorough discussion of agile, SCRUM, and XP methodologies and some advanced thinking about how to scale agile practices and *Lean Software* by Mary Poppendieck for the fundamental principles governing agile practices.

The potential benefits of an agile methodology implemented in concordance with the Agile Manifesto's core principles are compelling, especially in terms of delivery efficiencies and team morale. However, the role of the agile business analyst is still taking shape. To learn about how business analysis principles may be applied in an agile software development environment, study *Discover to Deliver: Agile Product Planning and Analysis* by Ellen Gottesdiener and Mary Gorman and the agile perspective outlined in Version 3 of the *Business Analysis Body of Knowledge* (anticipated in April 2015).

It is also important to note that variations of agile approaches exist, such as SCRUM, Extreme Programming, and Feature-Driven Development. Moreover, agile philosophies are not limited to software development practices. Lean methodologies are based on a collection of waste-minimizing and value-maximizing principles with roots in the manufacturing industry. Many practitioners now seek to apply lean principles in business contexts beyond manufacturing and software.

Significant philosophical and semantic debates over how to define these terms and processes prevail in many circles. Most of the differences revolve around development techniques and not core principles and have little direct impact on the business analyst. Before jumping head first into the debates, take some time to understand the terms that are being used and the context in which they are used. Many pundits

[5] Agile Manifesto. http://agilemanifesto.org/. 2001. Accessed 8/12/2014.

in business analysis and software development report that every ten or twenty years a new set of terms emerges to describe concepts that they have been applying on their most successful projects for a long, long time.

Mix And Match

Many organizations mix and match components of different methodologies to meet their organizational process needs. For example, as you are assessing job descriptions, you cannot assume that because an organization is requesting for its business analysts to write use cases that it has implemented the RUP. It may be documenting the use cases upfront using a waterfall process or using a use case to tie together a set of user stories to be delivered incrementally using an agile process. Some organizations consciously choose to use bits and pieces of different methodologies, and some believe that they have implemented a specific process but in reality have not fully implemented it.

With all of that said, treat this section as a guide to help you understand the possibilities, not to pigeon-hole an organization. You will understand the most about an organization's software development methodology by talking to the people who use it day-to-day or reading their process documentation.

Tools

Myriad different tools may used by business analysts. In just about every business analyst job and contract I have held, I have learned how to use at least one new tool, and it is not unusual to be exposed to several. Once you get beyond basic word processing and communication tools, the sheer number of toolsets available means that each organization will choose a set of tools that best supports its workflow and budget.

Rather than focusing on learning specific tools, it makes more sense to be aware of the types of tools that organizations use to optimize the requirements or software development processes. Over the course of your career, you will use many tools as a business analyst, and most of them are relatively easy to learn.

In this section, we will review the tools that are part of the business analyst workflow. We consider tools that business stakeholders use later on in the section about Domain-Specific Skills.

Word Processing, Spreadsheets, And Slide Decks

Microsoft Office® skills are required for most, if not all, office positions, and a business analysis position is no exception. Knowing the basics of Word, Excel, and PowerPoint is necessary. Knowing how to exploit advanced features may be necessary for specific positions. For example, a business analyst role with a heavy data analysis component would best be filled by a professional who is skilled in using Excel to sort and filter data and perhaps also in creating tables and charts or devising and running macros.

E-Mail

As a business analyst, you may also write, read, and respond to a lot of e-mails. You will probably send e-mails with attached documents for review or to coordinate meetings and collaboration. You will receive e-mails with questions from your stakeholders and developers. E-mail communication is a key skill, as is knowing when to pick up the phone or walk down the hall because an e-mail is not an appropriate way to address a particular question.

Requirements Management Tools

Requirements management tools are web-based or client-installed database applications that are used to support requirements management for a project or system. Requirements management tools provide a cohesive structure for tracking and tracing requirements and are used in organizations with formal and mature software development processes. Organizations not employing requirements management tools frequently store requirements in documents or spreadsheets on a shared drive or intranet document repository.

The features provided by requirements management tools vary widely. Some tools provide the most support in the upfront product development cycle and in vetting enhancement requests, and others are more integrated with the software delivery cycle.

The basic features of a requirements management tool may include the following:

- Capturing requirements
- Assigning attributes to requirements (such as priority, risk, and cost)
- Linking requirements (in hierarchies and across hierarchies)
- Analyzing the traceability of requirements
- Configuration management of the requirements
- Generating specifications or documents for review
- Inter-operability with other tools (such as design, modeling, and test case management tools)

For a comprehensive overview of the tools available and more detail about potential functionality offered, check out the INCOSE Requirements Management Tools Survey. [6]

Barring direct experience with a tool as a consumer or as an approver of requirements in a previous role, seek ways to familiarize yourself with the tools that occur again and again in job descriptions.

---

[6] http://www.incose.org/ProductsPubs/products/rmsurvey.aspx. Accessed 10/7/2014.

Many of the tools offer free trials. Downloading and exploring a tool that a potential employer uses can be an excellent way to gain some experience and familiarity with the generalities of a tool. Be aware that most of these tools are highly customizable, so each employer might use them a bit differently to support their requirements management process.

While on occasion a senior-level business analyst position will require or have a preference for expertise in a particular set of tools, it is doubtful that familiarity with a tool will make or break a manager's hiring decision for the vast majority of business analyst jobs.

Intranets And Document Management Tools

Historically, organizations used file folders for sharing documents that needed to be accessed by several people inside an organization. In my first business analyst job, we spent a considerable amount of time discussing how to layout folder structures on our projects and what our file-naming scheme should be.

Today, more organizations are using intranets or other types of document management tools to share documents. Still other organizations forego documents and organize requirements and project information in wikis.

In a more recent business analyst role, we used SharePoint to store all project-related information. We discussed how to organize our project folders and what to call each type of document. Fast forward a little more, and I am working in an organization that prefers to store project information in a wiki. Our discussions about organizing information focused on what pages to create in our wiki for each project and how to organize the collection of pages about each project.

Shared folders, document management tools, and wikis all enable people to access and update a shared set of information. As a business analyst, it is important to be aware of the different types of information management tools that exist and how the information you generate needs to be found and used in your organization.

Defect Tracking Tools

Defect tracking tools are also known as bug tracking or issue management tools. Whatever an organization calls them, they are essentially database applications that are used to manage issues with a system or project during the delivery cycle. It would be rare to find that the job requirements for a business analysis position include specific tool expertise, but you should understand the available features of defect tracking tools and be able to speak to how you might use them as a business analyst.

A business analyst might use these tools for the following activities:

- Follow-up on requirements defects
- Manage issues for a project or system
- Manage enhancement requests (in organizations without a requirements management tool)
- Log issues or defects discovered in user acceptance testing
- Prioritize defects

Project Management Tools

Project management tools take many forms, from scheduling and resource management tools such as Microsoft® Project to database-driven tools like Microsoft® Team Foundation Server and Rally Software®. A variety of web-based project management tools that provide basic requirements, issues, and project tracking capabilities are available as well and promote collaboration among team members. Collaborative tools are growing in popularity, and you are more liable to find them in smaller companies or organizations with less formal processes.

With such a broad range of tools available, it is rare to find a business analysis position requiring specific expertise unless it involves actual project management responsibilities.

Visual Modeling Tools

Many business analyst positions require visual modeling skills. Microsoft® Visio is by far the most popular tool you will find in job descriptions and is commonly used to build workflow diagrams, data models, and site maps. Enterprise Architect is a more fully-featured visual modeling tool that enables multiple business analysts to collaborate on models, integrates visual modeling and requirements management capabilities, and enables traceability between the requirements and developed and deployed code. A more sophisticated tool like Enterprise Architect may be used in organizations that also employ more formal modeling notations, such as UML.

In addition, business analysts use tools to produce wireframes, mock-ups, or prototypes. While Microsoft® Visio may be used to build wireframes or mock-ups of screens to be implemented as part of the application, several other types of tools are offered that make the wireframing process much more efficient.

The following is a short list of tools with free trials, making them useful resources to experiment with wire-framing concepts and page layout:

- Axure: http://www.axure.com
- Mockup Screens: http://MockupScreens.com
- Balsamiq: http://www.balsamiq.com

Even Microsoft® Word and PowerPoint provide some basic functionality for depicting the layout of a new screen.

A business analyst position that also includes more formal user interface design responsibilities might require Adobe® Photoshop or programming knowledge for creating functional user interface designs. While it may make sense to pair these two roles together, user interface and graphic design are outside the scope of the business analyst role as it is discussed in this book.

Domain-Specific Skills

Business analysts frequently ask me the same question, "It seems that every business analyst job I consider requires some area of business expertise that I do not have. How do I possibly become an expert at all of these different industries and domains?"

As a still-emerging profession, many business analyst jobs are organized around other business or technical domains, and related requirements work their way into job descriptions. It is not uncommon to see job requirements such as familiarity with a specific accounting system or a deep understanding of the insurance industry listed in a business analyst job description.

The answer to the question is that you do not need to become an expert in all of these different industries and domains to be successful as a business analyst. That would be nearly impossible. Instead, business analysts either choose to specialize in one domain or choose the generalist path, which focuses on jobs that value their business analyst skills over their domain-specific skills.

Domain-specific skills can help accelerate your progression into business analysis. Kimberley, one of my coaching clients, came to business analysis with an extensive professional network and expertise in the travel industry. Her first three business analyst contract positions were in companies within the travel industry, and her expertise was a major factor in getting the job and being successful. In those positions, she expanded her business analyst skills and, over time, she qualified herself for a broader range of business analyst jobs, including many generalist business analyst positions.

In Chapter 5 on business analyst roles, we will discuss how you can use your industry, functional domain, and functional tool expertise to your advantage in pursuing your business analyst career goals.

Putting It To Practice #4

Assess Your Business Analysis Skills

Congratulations on making it through this chapter! A ton of information is included here, and you might be feeling a bit overwhelmed. Let's break the information presented in this chapter into concrete, actionable steps that you can use to move forward in your business analysis career.

At the beginning of the chapter I asked you to keep track of two categories as you went through the list of skills. Now, let's organize what you have learned about your strengths in the core competencies, business analysis skills, and related skills.

Below are two steps to navigate.

1. Transcribe a list of core competencies and business analysis skill areas. (The Resource Pack that accompanies this book contains a worksheet that walks you through each of these steps so you do not have to write your list from scratch. You may download the Resource Pack for free by visiting the following link: http://www.bridging-the-gap.com/ba-resource-pack)

2. For each item on the list, assess your level of strength in this area. For example, you might break down each skill into the following levels of strength: know nothing, have basic knowledge, expert.

You can write out your assessment in your notebook or use the downloadable worksheet provided. Either way, you will leave this task better informed about your strengths and competencies.

As a side note, it is not uncommon for an experienced professional to go through a list like this and discover that they have been doing business analysis under a different job title and perhaps even using different terminology to describe their skills and deliverables. Sometimes the path to establishing a business analyst career is embracing the standards and practices within the profession and beginning to call yourself a business analyst.

✓ Putting It To Practice #5

Define A Skills-Improvement Plan

Look back through your list of skills and how you rated your strengths. Select three skill areas you would like to improve upon. These could be areas of weakness for you or areas that you found that you were relatively strong in but feel that you could be even stronger. Highlight your three skill areas.

For each highlighted skill area, brainstorm three steps you can take to improve your skills in this area. Examples might be reading an online article or a book, watching a webinar, or taking a course. (With the Skills Assessment worksheet, you will also receive online resource suggestions for each of the business analysis skill areas.)

Select between one and three tasks to complete in the next thirty days. We will circle back to this list when we discuss making a professional development plan, but by taking preliminary steps now, you will already have forward momentum by the time we get there.

CHAPTER 3

How To Expand Your Business Analysis Experience

Whether your dream is to be a star football player or a high-performance business analyst, the recipe to get there doesn't change: you must use deliberate practice to gradually get better at the skills that are important for your role. It is the steady accumulation of a related set of skills relevant to your craft that makes you become truly great at what you do.

~ Adriana Beal, Beal Projects

One of the most successful paths into business analysis involves accumulating relevant career experiences doing business analysis work, even while you are employed in a non-business analyst job.

Before we plunge into the ways that you may choose to expand your experience, let's look at my path to business analysis.

One day, a senior business analyst in my company mentioned that a new position was opening up soon. She recommended that I apply for it.

I was in quality assurance and dedicated to my current, always over-worked team, and I said, "Well, there is a lot going on. This might not be the right time."

To this day, I feel fortunate for her reply, "Well, when will be the right time? This would be a wise career move and probably more money too."

She gave me valuable advice. I took it to heart and applied for the position. Well over a decade later, I am still glad I did.

Upon reflection, this was not a chance meeting in a hallway. I had taken some actions that had qualified me to begin a career in business analysis.

- I participated in requirements and use case review meetings. I found errors. I questioned details. I helped make the requirements better by being a critical consumer.
- I established a new testing program to streamline the quality of an aspect of the system that was previously subject to ad hoc and unorganized testing from the business. I developed automated tests and organized business testing to define a structured User Acceptance Testing (UAT) process. I proactively helped the team resolve issues that surfaced in UAT. I was learning to plan, communicate, and analyze while also defining and improving a business process.
- I built strong product and stakeholder relationships within my company. As a quality assurance engineer, I had been involved in more than fifteen projects. I had worked with most of the project managers, product owners, business analysts, and developers.
- Through participating in those fifteen-plus projects, I had learned how our systems worked and come to know most of our products inside and out. This functional application expertise was a strength I drew on while leading requirements meetings.
- I had begun pursuing my master's degree in library and information science. Since our primary customer group was libraries and librarians, I was building expertise in the industry.

I did not learn the fundamentals of business analysis until I was employed as a business analyst. I was given the chance to learn business analyst skills on the job because of the experience and credibility that I had gained as a quality assurance engineer. It is doubtful that I would have found a business analyst position in another company at that time. But a year and a half later, after leading the business analyst effort on a few successful projects, I had become a well-qualified business analyst and landed a higher level and better paying position in another company.

This chapter is about helping you gain business analyst experiences and develop your core competencies to catapult yourself into a business analysis career. When you pay close attention to the work around you, you will see ways to take on business analysis responsibilities.

It is doubtful that these opportunities will land in your lap. Instead, be proactive in seeking out new work assignments. Talk to your manager. Talk to trusted colleagues. Volunteer to take on new responsibilities or tasks that no one else wants to do. Find out who needs help, and offer up your emerging skills and knowledge.

In the sections that follow, I have outlined the types of responsibilities that you may find, what the responsibility is, and how it helps you move your business analyst career forward. The tasks are divided into five sections:

- Responsibilities that apply in an extensive range of work situations
- Responsibilities frequently found for those in technical roles
- Responsibilities most often found for those in business functions
- Common job functions that you can re-frame as business analysis tasks
- What to do if your current organization is not an option

You may discover a relevant idea in a section that does not directly apply to your career situation, so I suggest reading the entire chapter. Through this process, you may also discover new business analysis experiences to add to your skills assessment.

Responsibilities That Apply In Many Work Situations

Let's view a few general responsibilities that apply in many work situations. While they are not as specific as the responsibilities that we will speak to later in this chapter, they are almost always present and so provide fast and easy ways to initiate your path to business analysis. Begin with one or two of the following ideas, and you will build momentum that makes the responsibilities we discuss later seem more promising.

Work With Business Analysts

Many professionals work with business analysts prior to becoming one. Leverage any occasion you have to observe business analysts or partner with them on a team. As you build relationships with other business analysts, let them know about your career goals. They may invite you to shadow them or help them with a business analysis task.

Remember that not everyone who does business analysis has the business analyst job title, so be broad. Consider alternate titles such as product manager, marketing analyst, process analyst, and operations analyst, as well as technology manager, project manager, and department head.

Consultants can also be a resource for you. If your company hires outside consultants for a software or process improvement project, an assortment of business analysis tasks will be accomplished. Put yourself in a position to contribute to the project or observe. Go to lunch with a consultant, linger after meetings, or catch them at the water cooler. Ask about their process. Get their perspective on the project and the organization.

In my second business analyst role, my organization hired a software consulting company to implement a new product. I faced a few particularly challenging analysis tasks, and the head of the consulting team, who operated in many business analysis capacities, suggested models that would help me analyze the problem. I also observed him leading technical design sessions using new techniques that I later applied to my own requirements sessions. My relationship with this team became so strong that after I decided to leave this position, the team lead let me know that he would have hired me if he had known that I was searching for a new job.

You can nearly always learn something from consultants, as they have experiences from across multiple organizations to share. No harm can come from building these relationships, and doing so may lead to learning new concepts, gaining a broader perspective, and even some attractive job prospects.

Facilitate A Meeting

Facilitating meetings is one of the most basic business analysis skills. The more experience you have running meetings, facilitating discussions, and publishing meeting notes, the more business analyst experiences you will accumulate.

For example, in my quality assurance engineer role I facilitated test plan reviews and bug triage meetings. Test plan reviews were similar to requirements reviews, and I developed many skills that helped me validate requirements as a business analyst. Bug triage discussions, where we evaluated and prioritized the open defects discovered during testing, were similar to the problem-solving and requirements prioritization tasks that I was responsible for as a business analyst.

You may be able to facilitate meetings within your department, on cross-functional teams, or for special committees.

Take Notes At A Meeting

It can be a challenge to facilitate a meeting and get all the notes down on paper. Even if you cannot find a meeting to facilitate, there could be an occasion to take notes. Offer to scribe for another meeting facilitator. It's doubtful that anyone will challenge you for this responsibility.

When you take on this responsibility, your listening skills will improve tremendously. You may also discover openings to ask questions, clarify what is being said, and present summaries, meaning that you will begin to be noticed as someone who can engage in business analysis work.

These ideas will get you underway, but it is possible to take on many more specific business analysis responsibilities as well. Let's examine the tasks available to those in technical roles next.

For Those In Technical Roles

One of our course participants, Wendy, was a software developer who wanted to be a business analyst. She participated in our Business Process Analysis course and realized that there were several processes within her software development team that needed documenting. She collaborated with her manager to select a process that would help the organization move forward. It turned out that there was an area of the customer set-up process that management was interested in automating. She documented the process.

Then she was asked to present the process to a group of managers. The management team was impressed with her documentation skills and how she presented herself. They approved the project.

After sharing her career goals with her manager, Wendy was invited to attend a customer meeting, a rare circumstance for software developers in this organization. Wendy again proved her listening and communication skills by asking relevant questions but not speaking using technical jargon.

While her organization had a product manager, this person needed help with requirements. Her manager promised to establish a business analyst role for her. It took a few months for agreement to become reality, and Wendy persisted in assuming business analyst work wherever she could. Eventually she was promoted into a new business analyst role conceived just for her.

Wendy's story highlights how someone in a technical role can take on several business analyst tasks. Technical roles may include software developer, programmer analyst, database administrator, quality assurance engineer, technical support person, and any other role where you are involved with technology day-to-day.

When you are in a technical role, watch for activities that move you closer to the business or open up possibilities to take a broader perspective on a problem or a solution. Let's observe the specific ways this process works.

Collaborate With Customers Or Stakeholders

Business analysts collaborate with customers and stakeholders, but many technical experts are not in direct contact with the people who use, sell, or market the results of their work. By engaging with customers and stakeholders, you will learn more about the domain-specific terminology and skills that are required to be on the business side. You will begin to understand why the software does what it does and how it is used by the business community. You will also be in a position to practice essential communication skills such as listening and asking questions.

Ask the business analyst or project manager if you can sit in on a requirements or project meeting. Ask a product manager if you can observe their next focus group or usability test. You could even individually ask a key business stakeholder out for lunch or coffee to learn more about their role.

Warning: If you have implemented or know a lot about the code in this system, you might be tempted to respond to observations and questions using technical jargon. When attending a meeting with business stakeholders, learn to see the system and process from the viewpoint of the people who use it.

Demo Software

Demoing a piece of software you have built or customized is another way to collaborate with customers and stakeholders. Put your defenses aside, and ask for honest feedback and new ideas. While demoing, you will see how thick your skin is and practice embracing feedback about your work. Throughout the demo, ask questions to get the perspective of others about the software and to better understand how it will be used.

Alternatively, outside of work, you could conduct a demo for a friend or professional contact. You will gain experience explaining your business and the product.

Become A Critical Consumer Of Requirements

Leverage your position as a consumer of requirements to learn more about the requirements process. You probably have already noticed that some requirements artifacts are much more helpful than others. If you are a developer, you may experience that some requirements are both clear and allow the freedom for you to make important implementation decisions. Other requirements constrain your efforts in challenging ways. As a quality assurance professional, some requirements make it apparent what and how to test, while others make it a challenge to identify what functionality would pass a test case.

Build on these insights to gain a deeper understanding of the requirements process and practice the skills business analysts use during requirements validation. Investigate why a certain type of requirements is most useful to you. Help the business analyst understand your perspective and possibly make adjustments. Business analysts respect perceptive questions and thoughtful analysis. If you can find something that they did not think of, and you bring it up in a respectful way, they will be grateful, and they will think highly of you.

Analyze A (Business) Process

Wendy's chance to initiate a business analyst career began with analyzing a software development process. Part of my path to business analysis involved clarifying, analyzing, and improving a test process. While it is easy to miss that software development and other technical processes are business processes, this responsibility provides one of the most effective paths into business analysis.

Analyzing a business process opens up the possibility of collaborating with stakeholders to understand the current-state and desired future-state processes. A stakeholder is anyone from the business or implementation team who is impacted by the project. In the case of a technical business process, other members of your technical team may be stakeholders in both senses of the term.

Build workflow diagrams and business process documentation to describe the process. As you validate the process, you will practice important communication and collaboration skills. Once you analyze the business process, the improvements you find may be addressed through new projects that require the full scope of business analysis activities.

Help Select New Software

Is your team or your business planning to select a new software package? If so, get involved in these projects in any way you can. Common software packages include project tracking, time tracking, bug/issue tracking, source control repositories, and intranet portals.

Offer to analyze multiple tools against your team needs. Many business analyst skills can be used to support even the smallest of projects.

- Interview your teammates to discover requirements.
- Analyze the process that the tool will support.
- Develop a features or requirements list to identify the business and/or functional requirements the new tool needs to fulfill.
- Conduct a gap analysis between the current state and the future state.
- Analyze how data will be migrated from the current state to the future state.

Be careful not to take advantage of the situation and make all of the decisions but instead focus on facilitating discussion and agreement between multiple team members.

Do Business Analyst Work

Many companies do not employ business analysts. Other companies employ too few business analysts for the number of projects they want to complete. Make a case for adding a business analyst to the staff (yourself), or help your company explore how this function would work by taking on a few business analyst tasks, such as a requirements document or the product backlog, for your next project.

When the software development process is fluid, you can make progress toward your business analysis career goals without gaining explicit buy-in for conceiving a new business analyst role. On any new project, invest some time in analysis and documentation before coding or testing. You could draft the requirements, formulate a test checklist, or summarize discussions in meeting notes. By completing these business analysis tasks, you will be helping to forge better project outcomes and move toward your career goals.

Solve A New Problem Or Create A New Benefit

Use your detailed knowledge of the tool or application to solve a new problem for your customer, or help them explore a new benefit. Take some of your own time to brainstorm what could be possible with the technology you have, decide how that might fit within the customer's perspective, and talk to people about your idea. Practice talking about the perceived benefit in non-technical jargon.

While the path from a technical role to business analysis is a common one, it is equally common for those in business functions to move into business analyst roles. Let's consider some of the responsibilities more commonly found for those in business functions next.

For Those In Business Functions

One of my biggest career moves occurred before I was in the quality assurance role I mentioned earlier. I was an assistant editor and assigned to work on one of our online content products. At a critical point of the project, the senior editor I was helping went on a three-week vacation. While attending project meetings in his stead, someone expressed concerns about how the content was being indexed. I volunteered to validate that the content was being searched and displayed correctly. Taking on this responsibility involved analyzing the requirements, defining a test plan, using a debugging tool, and producing a test results report. I had done none of these activities before, but I learned quickly.

By the time the senior editor returned, I had demonstrated my ability to work on technology projects, use new software, and present actionable bug reports to the technology team. Two months later I was offered the quality assurance engineer job, which, as we have seen, eventually led to my first business systems analyst job.

If you are employed in a business function, whether as a subject matter expert or an internal customer, close the gap between yourself and the technologies and systems that you use every day, obtain a broader perspective of these systems and the people who use them, or apply analysis techniques within the business processes of your department.

Become A Subject Matter Expert (SME) On A Project

Getting involved in a technology project that directly impacts your functional area will lead to many business analysis opportunities. Help the technology team craft a successful solution by envisioning the new application, providing input about your current processes, and providing your ideas about what the new system should do. Consider documenting process flows and business requirements.

If you are working with someone filling a business analyst role, ask to be involved in the requirements process. You can offer to help draft documentation, organize information, or perform other activities that help you step from the SME role into an analysis role. If you sense that the business analyst feels that you are stepping on their toes, be upfront about your career goals, and ask for their help in building some experience.

Be A Facilitator SME

As a subject matter expert, you have a lot of leeway in how you make decisions. If you routinely make decisions based on your own expertise, consider techniques for involving others, such as facilitating brainstorming sessions and observation. You might find your decisions improving while you work on your elicitation, facilitation, and communication skills.

Help Represent Another Department On A Project

Like a business analyst, an SME brings a special skill set to the project team, and helpful SMEs are hard to find. Not all groups have perfect candidates, or some groups are too over-worked to dedicate someone to a project. When a department's point of view is under-represented on a project, offer to take decisions to the department's members for consideration and take their input back to the implementation team. You will get practice eliciting, analyzing, communicating, and validating requirements.

Lead A Project In Your Department

Not all projects require a cross-functional team to analyze and implement them. Many projects happen inside a single department or when a handful of departments work closely together. Take a leadership role in a project such as organizing an area of the intranet, selecting a new software system to support your team, or analyzing and improving a business process.

Invest some time in analysis and documentation before implementing the solution. You could draft the requirements, generate a requirements checklist, or summarize discussions in meeting notes. When a project has a technology component, you may need to learn new technical jargon and perhaps even communicate with an outside vendor about your department's needs. You might also be able to define the project scope and requirements.

Facilitate A Process Improvement Session

Nearly all projects touch one or more business processes. Software projects automate business processes, and business analysis involves business process as much as software requirements. Our course participants have evaluated processes as diverse as on-boarding new employees, scheduling a workshop, reinstating a policy, planning a budget, and resolving customer issues.

Consider the processes that your department supports regularly, and seek out any confusing or error-prone processes. These are ripe areas in which to gain valuable business analysis experience by modeling the existing business process and facilitating sessions to determine how to improve the process. You will gain experience in analysis and collaboration techniques.

Help Conduct A Return On Investment (ROI) Analysis

If your company or department is considering a significant budgetary expenditure, it is a common practice to conduct a Return on Investment (ROI) analysis. Common examples include hiring a new full-time or temporary employee, licensing a new tool, or improving an existing process.

Help your manager or another leader assess the impact of the investment. This type of analysis will help you learn the importance of prioritization and will broaden your perspective regarding how your organization spends and makes money.

Become The Point Of Contact For Technical Issues

In most organizations, certain people within the business serve as the liaison with the technology team when issues arise, whether they are internal or external. Get involved in this process. Learn to clarify and validate issues before submitting them to the technology team. Help the technology team through the resolution process. You will learn a lot about how the systems work, be exposed to more technology, and may bridge the gap between the business and technical teams.

While it is doubtful that you have gotten to this point and not discovered one relevant opportunity, after working individually with many business analysts I have found that on occasion a client feels that their employment situation is too rigid to enable them to take on new tasks. In the next section, you will learn how to re-frame your current position using a business analysis mindset and build momentum toward bigger business analysis responsibilities.

How To Re-Frame Your Current Tasks

Your employment situation may not provide the flexibility required for you to volunteer for new tasks, but that does not necessarily mean that you cannot gain business analysis experience. Instead, re-frame your current work as business analysis work.

Remember the underlying core competencies we discussed earlier:

- Problem-Solving and Critical Thinking
- Analytical Thinking
- Relationship-Building
- Self-Management
- A Thick Skin
- Driving Improvements
- Communicating

And the core business analysis skill areas:

- Collaboration Techniques
- Requirements Specifications
- Diagrams and Visual Models

You do not necessarily need to take a project from beginning to end as a business analyst to gain business analysis experience. Each of these areas provides many fruitful means for re-framing an activity in terms of the business analysis role. Be resourceful, and brainstorm ways to piece together experiences.

Let's review some tactics you might use to re-frame your current work within a business analysis context.

Practice Listening

The most critical skill you can refine and develop with respect to conducting requirements sessions is listening. Listening means comprehending what you hear and letting the stakeholder know that you have understood them.

You can practice this skill using a technique called paraphrasing. After listening to someone speak on a topic, repeat what they said back to them in your own words. You will receive immediate feedback about how well you understood what the person meant. Use this technique repeatedly to improve your listening skills.

Practice Translating

Many disagreements about project scope and requirements can be traced back to stakeholders not using consistent terminology. As you improve your listening skills, you will begin to notice disconnects in conversations where people are saying the same thing using different words.

Practice re-framing what each person is saying to help them all understand each other better. When disagreements arise, ask each person to define their terms. You may be able to facilitate a more productive discussion and gain agreement about a go-forward approach.

Practice Asking Questions

Regardless of whether you are responsible for facilitating a discussion, a well-placed question can serve to re-frame the discussion and help others communicate. Ask questions when something is not clear or if people appear to be talking past one another.

Observe Someone

Observation provides the occasion to practice skills that business analysts use during elicitation, such as learning new systems, asking questions, and analyzing a process. When you learn a new process or system as part of your work, it is not uncommon for a trainer or team expert to demo the new solution or sit down with you one-on-one. As the trainee, you are observing.

You make the choice whether to be an active or passive observer. Business analysts are naturally active observers who ask questions, take notes, and connect the dots. Do the same, and you will be exercising business analysis core competencies.

As a side note, this means that any new responsibility you take on becomes a business analysis opportunity for you. As an editor, when I offered to validate that content was being searched and displayed properly, I needed to learn to use a debugging tool. A technical trainer offered me one-on-one training. I asked questions until I exhausted her knowledge of the tool and how it was used. I went on to establish an improved validation process and make a notable contribution to the project team. As mentioned earlier, this experience was a career catalyst that eventually led to an offer to work on the quality assurance team.

Develop A Systems And Processes Mindset

Business analysts think clearly about who does what and how processes are accomplished within an organization. Develop a thorough understanding of how your organizations works, and you will notice ways to expand your business analysis experience.

- Do you know who is responsible for what and what the primary goal of each department is?
- Do you know how information flows through your organization?
- Do you understand the business processes at work within your organization?

Comb your organization's intranet and other internal information resources for organizational charts, training materials, and process documentation that will help you see the big picture. Inspect external communications such as your website, marketing materials, and customer communications to see your organization's processes from the outside in.

If you are an analytical thinker, it would be difficult to complete this research and not find at least a few improvement ideas.

Improve Something

Take on a mindset of continuous improvement within your department or organization, and you will enhance your critical thinking skills while also learning to sell your ideas. You can improve a process, a template, or a piece of communication. Improvements may be big or small.

Consider the value of each improvement you make and how it impacts others within your organization. Share the improvement with others.

Scope A Project Or Activity

The concept of scope applies in many circumstances outside of formal projects. Job descriptions represent scope. Any new task you take on has scope, regardless of whether it is explicitly defined and written down.

Use these types of assignments to practice scoping a project. Write a one-page document or an e-mail describing the scope of the project, task, or initiative. Send it to your manager or other participants to confirm a mutual understanding.

Develop Use Case Thinking

Developing use case thinking helps improve your analysis and critical thinking skills. A use case is a format that business analysts use to describe functional requirements for software systems. Everyday situations usually benefit from a bit of use case analysis.

For example, given the number of systems and software that are integrated to watch television, using the remote control to watch a specific show or movie can involve a complex set of tasks. The set of steps necessary to watch a show or a movie could be analyzed using a use case format, along with alternate flows for watching a DVD and an exception flow for handling the scenario when your wireless internet needs to be re-set.

Participants in our course on use cases are frequently surprised at the far-reaching applicability of the technique and how it makes them better at analyzing problems. Once they write a use case as part of the course, they begin seeing use cases everywhere in their home and work environments and structuring some of their more complicated thinking around use cases.

Host A Review Or Demo

We conducted reviews and demos in early childhood. The only difference is that we called it show and tell. Professionals keep showing and telling today in a number of capacities, whether it be to demonstrate what they have accomplished to an executive committee, train others on a new process, or answer a question.

You might already be participating in meetings that include reviews or demos. In this case, improve your demos by clarifying the observer's perspective before the meeting and customizing your demo to meet their needs. This will help you become more externally focused and open to feedback.

Get Involved

Finally, because career breaks happen for those who seek out new experiences, keep your eyes open for any chance to work with others, especially with people outside your immediate team or department. Join any team you can. Volunteer to serve on special committees.

When working on a team or committee, make contributions by taking on specific responsibilities. Remember that the career-changing experience that led to my invitation to join the quality assurance team came from stepping in to be part of a cross-functional team. I got noticed by a new set of people in my organization for my ability to add value. You can do the same.

When Your Current Organization Is Not An Option

Many of our readers and course participants know that they want to start a career in business analysis but are not currently employed. Others find their current organization so rigid that they are not able to make much headway or take on business analyst responsibilities as quickly as they would like. Even outside of formal employment, you can increase your confidence in your business analysis skills and expand your business analysis experience.

Volunteer Your Time

Nearly every organization benefits from business analysis, yet many organizations are either too small to hire a business analyst or do not have the funds. By volunteering your time on a limited basis, you may be able to practice a new skill, bolster your resume, and even gain valuable references.

While you can volunteer for any organization, the best opportunities tend to surface for small businesses or non-profit organizations. Contrary to what you might think, even non-profits need *business* analysts.

For example, one unemployed business analyst volunteered to analyze the business process her church was developing to recruit new volunteers. Another analyst interviewed his wife to gain insights into the budgeting process for a parent-teacher organization she led. Then he followed up and documented what he learned in a business process.

Another one of our course participants volunteered at a local business. She helped a pharmacy discover why there were so many errors when it filled prescriptions. The owner of the pharmacy was well-connected locally and offered to provide references to several of her target companies.

If you are searching for a new job, volunteering provides a bonus of new and recent work experience as a business analyst that you can add to your resume. Contrary to what many professionals expect, you do not need to list volunteering in a special section or even note that your work was unpaid. In your work history section, include the name of the organization you worked for, give yourself a fitting title, and describe the work you did and the value you added in a few bullet points.

In some cases, volunteering can also lead to paid work. When a company benefits from your contribution, someone there may decide that they can afford to hire you as an employee or contractor.

Go Back In Time

Another way to increase your confidence in your business analyst skills is to re-visit projects or deliverables from past work experiences and apply business analyst techniques to them. One technologist saw how use cases could have helped his previous technical team flesh out more requirements earlier in the design process. He composed a couple of sample use cases analyzing the technology requirements that he had implemented in his most recent position. He even sent a sample to his previous manager with a suggested approach for utilizing the use case.

It is possible that such initiative could lead to being re-employed to help improve a process in an organization where you previously worked. In this case, our participant was able to speak more confidently in job interviews as to how the work he had done fit within the context of business analysis and how he would deploy a use case approach in the future. A few months later, he landed a business analyst job where his role was to coach others on applying use cases.

Apply Business Analysis At Home

Many business analysis techniques can be applied outside of work. Many of our job-seeking course participants analyze the process of searching and applying for jobs. Others analyze tools that they use, such as devising a use case to analyze Amazon's shopping cart. Still others use the techniques to improve their home life.

Below are a few examples of how to apply business analyst techniques at home:

- Before making your next major purchase (car, house, or even a blender), complete a requirements analysis. List out the features you want. Prioritize them. Compare your options against the features, balancing cost against benefits.
- Re-work an existing or broken process that is integral to running your household. Identify the beginning and the end.

Identify your desired outcomes from the process. Analyze the detailed tasks using flow charts. Search for optimization or even automation possibilities. Complete a new proposed process, and see the change through with your family or friends.

- Choose to purchase one piece of new software to use at home (taxes, television, or cataloging your library). Define your requirements and inventory options.

While these ways of practicing are not experiences you can add to your resume, they do help you gain confidence in your skills and can be beneficial practice.

✓ Putting It To Practice #6

Expand Your Business Analyst Experiences

Brainstorm ideas for how you can take on business analysis tasks in your current employment (or non-employment) situation. Once you run out of inspiration, study your Skills Assessment for additional ideas. Come up with at least ten or twenty suggestions.

Go through the list, and pick one that feels the most comfortable but represents something you have not done before. Develop an action plan for achieving it in the next two weeks.

Now, select one that feels like a stretch and that you feel will help you learn the most. Clarify it. Visualize yourself doing it. Think about how it would feel to do it successfully. Imagine how proud you will be of yourself when you make it happen. Make a note, and come back in a week or two and develop an action plan.

✓ Putting It To Practice #7

Record Your Business Analyst Experiences

For each business analyst experience you have, enter it into your notebook, explaining what you did and the impact it had on your organization. Describe how the task is a business analyst experience.

Consider these questions:

- Was the outcome positive or negative?
- What did you learn?
- What did you do well?
- What could you have done better?
- Now that you have done this, what else seems possible?

The Resource Pack contains a template for recording your business analyst experiences. Some have saved this template to their desktop and now review and update their experiences on a daily or weekly basis. (As a reminder, you may download the Resource Pack for free by visiting the following link: http://www.bridging-the-gap.com/ba-resource-pack.)

I cannot stress how important it is to reflect upon your experiences. Writing about the business analyst responsibilities you are undertaking will clarify your accomplishments and help you to gain insights that you would not have otherwise, which helps accelerate your transition. You will also develop material to add to your resume or discuss with your manager. As you write, you will surface new approaches for applying business analysis in your work or adjusting the work you are already doing so it aligns with business analysis.

✓ Putting It To Practice #8

Kick Off A Cycle Of One Business Analyst Experience Leading To Another

Come back to this task after you have gotten your feet wet with some business analysis experiences and built some confidence. Putting It To Practice #6 was specifically designed to help you select some tasks inside your comfort zone so you can build some confidence about your business analysis abilities. However, staying in your comfort zone will not necessarily propel your business analyst career forward.

Now you want to develop a plan to gain a broad base of business analysis experiences that will eventually qualify you for a business analyst position.

First, list the experiences that you have accumulated. Now, categorize them by the business analysis knowledge areas:

- Collaboration Techniques
- Requirements Specifications
- Diagrams and Visual Models

Does this help you identify any gaps? If so, focus your next tasks on filling these gaps.

Another way to identify gaps would be to review the knowledge areas in which you did not feel confident in your understanding. By now you may have done some reading of online articles or books to help you learn more about some areas. Now that you know more, find ways to practice your skills. Continue to evolve this plan as you rack up experiences and build momentum.

It is at this point in your career transition that professional training or hiring a coach or mentor may be exceedingly helpful. Training can help you build confidence as you apply business analysis techniques in your work. A coach or mentor can also help you develop a personalized plan and stay motivated to keep on track even when you face difficulties or obstacles.

The next chapter is about networking. As you begin meeting more business analyst professionals, you might consider asking one of them to be a mentor.

CHAPTER
4

How To Connect With Business Analyst Professionals

I learned more in the last year and a half than I would have in ten without social media.
~ Jonathan Babcock, Practical Analyst

Professional networking is an inexpensive, productive way to learn more about the business analysis profession. When you network professionally, you meet people who provide new insights, stay up-to-date about the profession, and discover new tactics to move your career forward. The majority of us network too little, and doing so leaves you exposed to being uninformed about what is happening outside your organization and unprepared for changes occurring in the profession.

Your goals for networking could include:

- Learning about the business analyst profession.
- Understanding the state of the profession in your location or target location.
- Establishing mutually beneficial relationships with other professionals.
- Contributing to the professional community.
- Finding your next position.

Finding your next position is, by necessity, last on the list. Many people focus their networking on short-term goals such as finding a job and lose out on the long-term career gains to be had. Instead, focus your efforts on the first four suggestions, and allow finding a position to be a by-product of these other activities.

Of course, you may let people know that you are seeking a new job, but do not make it the object of your conversations. When people meet you and are impressed with you as a person and a professional, they will let you know about vacancies you may be interested in.

Putting It To Practice #9

Set Your Networking Goals

Before jumping in to the how and what of professional networking, take a few minutes to write down what you would like to accomplish through networking. You can use the goals listed above, but it will be more meaningful if you re-classify those goals to suit your personal situation. Make them more specific to you.

It may be worthwhile to reflect on what you have done so far. What have you learned about yourself through the experiences you have had? Consider professional networking a means to build on the strengths you have identified or fill in some of your knowledge or experience gaps.

Once you get underway, the activities listed in this chapter may absorb a lot of time. Taking a few minutes to clarify and focus helps you to get the most out of this time-intensive activity and prioritize your investments.

Pay It Forward

In any sort of networking activities, always keep the concept of pay it forward close to heart. While much of what we will be talking about in this chapter speaks to what you personally have to gain by participating in specific networking activities, keep your eyes and ears open for contributions you can make. Seek out ways to help someone else, even if you will not receive a direct and immediate benefit. Give without the expectation of receiving in return. With this mindset, career prospects will open up for you.

As you converse with people, do not simply focus on what you want to learn, but find a pain point or a need with which you can help the other person out. Always watch for ways to make a contribution back to an organization or a relationship. Here are some ways to figure out what you can do to help another person:

- Listen carefully for needs and wants.
- Ask if there is anything you can do to help.
- Make generous, relevant offers to show your intentions.

You might think that since you are new in the profession you have little to offer. However, when you commit yourself to paying it forward, you will be amazed at the contributions you are able to make and doors that will open for you as a result of even the slightest of offerings.

Consider the following ways you may be able to assist others:

- Introduce two people who would benefit from meeting each other.
- Review an article, paper, or resume.
- Mock-interview a fellow colleague seeking a new position.
- Send relevant information to someone (such as a website, article, or book recommendation).

- Show gratitude. Taking the time to write a personal thank you (via e-mail or a traditional thank you card) for something you learned or how you value the services someone provided to you can be a reward in and of itself.

Be confident that you have something to give and that it has value. You do. You have power beyond measure to help other people.

Putting It To Practice #10

Decide What You Have To Offer

Nothing commits you to making an offer more than having prepared a list of ideas. Take a few minutes and brainstorm ways that you can help others.

Connect With Other Professionals At Local Events

Attending local professional events is an easy way to meet other professionals who are active in the community.

How To Find Events In Your Local Area

Professional associations have local chapters that hold professional meetings, and attending a couple of meetings is a fantastic way to learn more about the organization and the type of professionals who attend. If your local area has a chapter of the International Institute of Business Analysis™ (IIBA®), attend those meetings. To find out, go to the IIBA website (http://www.iiba.org), and browse the list of chapters. Most chapters have their own website with a list of historical and upcoming events.

Contrary to what many new business analysts assume, being employed as a business analyst, certified as a business analyst, or being an association member are not pre-requisites for attending a local chapter meeting. Most chapters allow non-members to attend for a modest meeting fee, which can range from $5 to $25.

If you do not have an IIBA chapter locally, research professional meetings in related professions, including business process engineering, product management, project management, quality assurance, or software development. It is quite probable that you will find business analysts at these other meetings. If you meet other local business analysts, taking the initiative to form your own IIBA chapter will help you gain credibility locally and meet additional people.

Professional associations are not only organized around job roles. Process-specific groups also exist. In particular, Agile and SCRUM tend to have local groups, and people from a broad range of software development disciplines attend these meetings. Also consider industry-specific groups where you will meet people from different professions but who work in the same industry. These groups could be especially helpful if you plan to leverage your industry expertise to help you transition into a business analyst role. In addition, many functional domains have associations, and many functional applications have user group meetings. Essentially, any area of expertise you have or are pursuing could lead you to a local professional event where you will meet others also interested in that topic.

Finally, if you are currently unemployed or have a lot of flexibility in your schedule, also research local career or job networking groups in your area. These groups help people in between jobs stay connected and up-to-date.

Several valuable resources are available for finding local events, most of them online. Below are a few of my favorites:

- Meet-up: http://www.meetup.com. This site allows local groups and organizers to post events for a small fee.

You will find numerous groups, not all of them geared toward professional topics.

- Local LinkedIn groups.
- Web searches for your location and *networking events* or *groups* or *meetings.*

Once you attend a few events, it will be easier to keep up-to-date and informed. Ask attendees what other meetings they go to. As an aside, if you are anything like I was when I first began networking, knowing what to talk about was the most difficult part of meeting new people. You now have a topic to talk about at your first event, and in what follows you will discover many additional conversation-starting ideas so you will never be at loss for words again.

How To Get The Most Out Of A Local Event

Many people are intimidated by networking meetings. I have never been well-versed at meeting new people, but since I became an independent consultant, I have learned a few techniques for turning these meetings into positive experiences.

First, it is critical to lower your expectations. We make networking meetings more difficult when our expectation (or hope or goal) is to find a job or make several perfect connections. Setting such an unrealistic goal will not only cause ongoing disappointment, but it will cause you to initiate inappropriate conversations and actually make that outcome less likely. Instead, set a reasonable expectation of say, meeting one person with whom you would like to have a more involved conversation and obtaining their contact information. As you reflect on the meeting, take pride in who you met and what you learned. Even if the encounter was not perfect, you probably learned at least one new thing, or it prompted you to think about something differently.

Make the effort to introduce yourself to at least one or two new people. Force yourself to do this, if necessary. Some groups are tight, and most people know each other. Other groups have just as many first-timers as regulars. Ask a few people some basic questions, such as:

- Is this your first meeting?
- Have you been here before? What's it like?
- Are you familiar with the speaker? Are you familiar with the topic?
- What do you do?
- How did you find that job? (You will learn so much by making this question a habit whenever anyone mentions a new job, a new contract, or a new anything.)
- What methodologies do you use?

When you meet someone interesting, explain your situation, and ask if they would be willing to meet with you and share their experience in more detail.

A professional meeting typically begins with time for open networking, then moves to the formal meeting with chapter announcements, and finally allocates an hour or more to a presentation by an expert speaker on a business analysis topic. At some meetings, recruiters and other hiring professionals will be there to speak about openings and meet candidates.

Be sure to plan adequate time to make the most of the event. Since most networking tends to happen before the presentation commences, arrive early. Also, plan to linger after the presentation concludes. After evening meetings, people tend to rush out to get back home to their families. I am always surprised at this because the topic of the presentation can make it easier to initiate conversations by asking what others thought about the presentation generally or a specific point. The people who linger want to meet people, so do not be tentative about opening a conversation about what the presenter had to say.

Take the time to follow up with who you meet. The next morning, e-mail anyone you met, noting an interesting aspect of your conversation and expressing your interest in meeting them to share their experiences. If you can attach something of value, say a link to a website or the title and author of a book you recommended, all the better. E-mailing each person helps him or her remember you and increases your chances of speaking again.

Putting It To Practice #11

Plan Your Professional Event Calendar

It is time to find networking events that you can attend in the coming months. If you are currently employed and relatively satisfied, a suitable goal might be to find an average of one or two events per month. If you are currently unemployed or want to find a new position in the next three months, consider setting a goal closer to two events per week.

A reasonable goal within each meeting would be to find one person with whom you would like to speak further, getting their contact information, and requesting the meeting. Keep reading to learn more about what to do in that meeting, in the Informational Interviews section.

Regardless of how many events you attend per week, focus on quality over quantity. Quality connections. Quality conversations. Quality learning from the presentations.

Leveraging The Connections You Already Have

In addition to meeting new people, it is quite possible that you already know people (or know people who know people) who can help you learn more about the business analysis profession and related topics.

Consider the following ideas to identify potential connections:

- Do you know any business analysts? Have you worked with anyone who held business analysis responsibilities in the past?
- Ask colleagues and friends if they know of anyone who might be interested in sharing their experience.
- Ask everyone you meet if they can recommend anyone else you should speak with. People may be willing to introduce you to a colleague or their manager, especially if they know that you are focused on learning, helping, and will be respectful of the person's time.
- Broadcast a request on LinkedIn or other online networking website. (We will talk more about online networking later in this chapter.)

The PathFinder[7] contains an excellent exercise called *The Networking Game.* It essentially asks you to list everyone you know personally and professionally, rate them based on how committed they are to your success, and identify how they might be able to help you. Walking through this process broadens your mind about the people you know, helps you become intentional about your networking, and helps you adjust to the idea of asking for appropriate help.

---

[7] *The Pathfinder: How to Choose or Change Your Career for a Lifetime of Satisfaction and Success.* Nicholas Lore. Pages 337-345.

Putting It To Practice #12

Set Up Informational Interviews

Contact two or three business analysts you already know or can be introduced to, and ask if they would be willing to share their experiences. Explain that you are considering pursuing a career in business analysis and would like to ask them a few questions about their experience in the profession.

Conduct Informational Interviews To Deepen Connections

The informational interview provides a fitting next step to initiate or build on a relationship. People love to talk about themselves, and you want to learn about being a business analyst.

Megan Herlihy successfully made the transition from marketing communications to business analysis. She started in her comfort zone by asking former colleagues for informational interviews and eventually graduated to asking people she met at networking events. One of the keys to her success was to focus on interviewing people she really found value in meeting. Megan interviewed one or two people per week for a few months and reports that 80 to 90 percent of the people she asked agreed to meet with her.

When you meet someone that you connect with, ask if you can e-mail them or call them to talk a bit more about what they do. Let them know that you are evaluating whether business analysis is the right career choice for you or that you are interested in learning more from successful business analysts and that you would appreciate the opportunity to ask them a few questions.

Conduct as many informational interviews as you possibly can. You will learn something different from everyone, even if it is simply the advantage of a new perspective. As you build experience interviewing business analysts, consider expanding your interviews to other professions to gain outside perspectives about business analysis.

When setting up an informational interview, be as flexible as possible with the other person. If it is reasonable, offer to meet them in their office, over their lunch hour, or outside their normal working hours for coffee or breakfast. I consider coffee meetings the best alternative as the cost of a coffee is nominal. You can either pick up both coffees or not, but it is not an economical inconvenience either way. Another option is to find a local library with private meeting rooms that you can reserve. Phone meetings are also a viable option and are especially useful when time is tight.

The questions you ask should be personal, in the sense that you are personally interested in the answers, but also professional, in that you should not ask someone you just met on a professional level questions they may not be comfortable answering.

You will get the most out of this activity if you develop a list of questions that address your knowledge gaps and business analyst experiences you are seeking. For example, if you have no experience with requirements management tools, you might consider asking your interviewees what tools they have used and what the merits were of each. Consider questions that will help you experience business analysis jargon and receive some informal training.

Alternatively, if you feel that you are a strong listener, you might want to ask how they use listening skills in their day-to-day work, providing you with more ideas for gaining business analysis experiences or re-phrasing experiences you have already had in business analyst language.

Below are the questions Megan used in her interviews, along with a few of my own suggestions:

- What are the main responsibilities of a business analyst? What is a work day like?
- What are the pros/cons of being a business analyst? Is there growth in this field?
- Who does a business analyst report to?
- Who does a business analyst work with?
- How would you describe the ideal candidate for a business analyst position? What skills are required?
- Why did you decide to become a business analyst?
- How did you find your first business analyst job?
- What business analysis training have you taken? What training would you recommend to someone in my position?
- What business analyst resources (websites, books, or training classes) would you recommend?
- What software development models are you familiar with (Waterfall, Agile)? Which do you prefer? Why?
- What local meetings do you attend? What are the benefits of them?
- What kinds of tools should a new business analyst learn about?
- How else do I find additional information? Who would you suggest I contact?

Putting It To Practice #13

Prepare For Your Informational Interviews

You may already have a few meetings set up. To get the most out of these meetings, take some time to prepare. You already have a list of skills you want to work on or ideas for experiences you want to build. You also have a list of concerns from the Pros and Cons list you completed at the end of Chapter 1. Use these lists and identify questions you have about getting started or areas where the perspective of a seasoned business analyst would help you take another step forward.

Once you have a list of topics, personalize your questions to the person you are interviewing. Review their LinkedIn profile and any information readily available through a web search. Think up a few questions specifically suited to their background and experience.

Alternatively, Ask A Question

You might be daunted by the idea of asking someone to set aside half an hour or more of their time to answer the questions you have about the profession. Or, you might have a question or two to ask someone who is extremely busy and difficult to schedule.

Luckily, Sheryl Sandberg suggests an alternative to the informational interview in *Lean In*. Instead of requesting an interview, ask the person one specific question. This strategy works best if the person is uniquely qualified to answer the question and you could not readily find the answer through your own research. It also helps if you have a compelling reason to ask the question and a means to benefit from learning the answer. When the question is specific and the person you ask is in a unique position to give you a response, the question itself demonstrates that you are thoughtful and being considerate of the other person's time.

For example, *what requirements tools are used by business analysts?* is a generic question that you could easily answer on your own. You could find such a list using a series of thoughtful web searches. However, you might ask a business analyst who recently completed a selection process a question such as, *I am taking on a new project to evaluate new requirements management tools, and I want to be sure that I would be helping the organization make an informed decision. Would you mind sharing the top three selection criteria you used to evaluate tools during your recent selection process?* You might add, *Were there any vendors who surprised you in a negative or positive way?* Unlike the list of tools used by business analysts, these questions ask for this specific person's expertise on a specific topic.

As Sandberg points out, a pattern of asking relevant, thoughtful questions of specific people you know and respect is one way to seek out mentoring support from your community. What is more, when you have shared interests, asking meaningful questions periodically can lead to a deeper and ongoing mentoring relationship between you both.

Online Networking

Another valuable way to expose yourself to new ideas and people is to network online. An abundance of websites and social networks are available, catering to nearly every profession and niche interest. People who join these networks are likely to be in search of like-minded individuals with whom to share ideas. By participating in a few online networks you will build an online profile of yourself as a professional business analyst.

An additional benefit of participating in online networking communities is that you can control your online presence. Recruiters and hiring managers frequently search online about candidates before making hiring decisions. If you have not already, put your name into any web search engine. You want your search results to sell you as a professional.

A few comments on blogs and publicly available forums can put some relevant, insightful information about you in these search results. These comments show that you are contributing to your own professional development by making use of the available resources.

Finally, if you are open to or specifically seeking to relocate, you might focus more attention on online networking activities to connect with people in your target location(s). Imagine moving to a new city and already knowing several professionals in the area. This is exactly what happens when you consciously network ahead of your relocation.

Social Networks

Not all social networks are equal, and no one network will offer everything you might be seeking. Explore multiple options and find the sites that best sync with your online inclinations.

Below is a short list of social networking sites that focus on business analysis and related topics:

- http://www.modernanalyst.com
- http://community.theiiba.org
- http://stickyminds.com

Start with these websites to get a feel for what the business analysis profession is doing online. Within them you will find profiles of individuals, links to blogs and other sites, links to companies that serve the business analysis profession, and much more.

Another wonderful resource for online discussions and links to articles is LinkedIn (http://www.linkedin.com). The power of LinkedIn for interacting with other professionals is in the groups. As of this writing, the following groups were productive and active in the business analyst space:

- International Institute Of Business Analysis
- Modern Analyst
- Agile Business Analyst

You may also want to check out the Bridging the Gap group that I manage.

Finally, business analyst communities have developed within broader social networking sites. Consider the following ways to find and network with business analysts:

- Twitter: check out individuals who post under the hashtag #baot or #iiba.
- Google Plus: use the term business analyst in the search bar to find relevant posts and people to connect with.
- Facebook: explore groups and pages about business analysts. Many of the business analyst blogs mentioned below also host Facebook groups or pages.

On any social networking website, some primary usage patterns occur. You will find members who:

1. Use the site to stay up-to-date and learn new things by consuming information.
2. Use the site to market their products, services, or content by broadcasting information.
3. Use the site to publicly communicate with others.

As you explore any social media platform as part of your professional development and online professional profile building, consider the following guidelines:

- Give people a reason to connect with you. Be interesting. Post interesting information. Share interesting experiences.
- If you want to carry on a lot of personal or what might be considered unprofessional chatter, strongly consider two profiles. Your comments show up in search results too. Even if you have two profiles, be careful what you share!
- Confirm that what you share resonates with your professional personality and how you would want potential employers and co-workers to view you. They may be reading.

Social media can be a productive part of establishing and maintaining connections. When I connect with people in my local area I tend to have a better idea of what they are up to in between face-to-face meetings, bringing a stronger connection to even infrequent in-person meetings.

Most social networks have forums, and this is an easy place to get to know a site. Reading the archives will give you a sense of the conversations. You can lurk for a while, but it is through active participation that you will receive the most value out of online networking. So graduate from watching to liking content, asking questions, responding to questions, sharing resources, and posting other comments. You will learn so much more and think so much more clearly when you capture your thinking in textual form and expose it to the community for response and feedback.

When participating on social networks, you can make it easy for others to get in touch with you. When commenting on a blog or forum, enable people to find out more about you and contact you by including a URL. If you do not have your own website or blog, link to your LinkedIn profile.

Make Individual Connections

General information and discussions are useful, and you can learn a lot online, but the real power of online networking comes when you make one-to-one connections with individuals.

When you encounter someone online that you share particular interests with or have interesting online dialogue with, send them a personal message. Most social networking sites have a way to send another member an e-mail through the site. If you cannot get in touch with the person through the site you are on, check and see if they have a LinkedIn profile. Most people do and set their profiles to enable them to receive message from other members, even if you are not connected.

Take care in crafting your e-mails. Begin with a sentence or two thanking them for some value they have provided or summarizing your interest based on discussions that have been made in these public forums. Then ask a question or two that you are legitimately interested in.

When you receive a response, which will happen more often than you expect, continue the dialogue either via e-mail or phone. These new contacts offer a terrific way to conduct informational interviews with a broader set of people than may be available in your locale or that may show up at the same networking events that you do.

Another way to find interesting people online is to search for professionals in your area with related job titles. Contact them directly, explaining your situation and asking if they would be willing to meet you and share their experiences.

You can also use LinkedIn to find non-local individuals and to schedule a phone conversation. This might be necessary if you are truly in a remote area. Otherwise, limit this type of extended search to people with whom you share multiple commonalities, for example if they made the transition to business analysis from the same career you are currently in or you share a common industry background. Well-targeted and thoughtful contacts through LinkedIn have a much higher success rate than haphazard form letters.

Websites And Blogs

Websites and blogs augment social networking sites by providing forums for one or more individuals to publish their ideas. Several websites about business analysis publish content, and you can learn about nearly any topic by reading online articles, white papers, and blog posts or listening in to podcasts and webinars. Reading web content is an excellent way to connect with other business analysts, learn from real-life experiences, and participate in discussions about current topics.

As you participate on one or more social networks, you will naturally become more aware of other online websites because many professionals share links to content on their own websites or websites they like. What follows is a short-list of high-quality websites by business analysts about business analysis. The writing available in this space is expanding every day.

- Business Analysis Times, a collection of articles by well-established business analysts in the industry: http://www.batimes.com
- Bridging the Gap, the article website I host: http://bridging-the-gap.com
- The Business Analyst Coach, an impressive podcast that shares interviews with business analyst professionals across the industry: http://www.thebacoach.com
- Modern Analyst, a collection of articles, blog posts, and directories of other resources for analysts: http://www.modernanalyst.com

- Practical Analyst by a working business analyst manager, Jonathan Babcock: http://practicalanalyst.com
- Requirements Defined, hosted by Seilevel, a professional services organization focused on creating software requirements: http://requirements.seilevel.com/blog (Seilevel's message board may also be a valuable resource.)

Putting It To Practice #14

Update Your Online Profiles

Take stock of the online profiles you already have, and consider how they would be viewed by potential employers or other professionals. Your online professional profiles should clearly state your career intentions and represent your professional persona. Take some time and clean up your profiles, paying special attention to your LinkedIn profile.

Putting It To Practice #15

Your Online Information Routine

Begin incorporating online business analyst activities into your daily or weekly routine. Check out the resources mentioned in this section that interest you the most. Leave a few comments or even initiate a discussion. Test the waters, and join in the community.

As you explore, select at least two to three resources to become part of your online information routine. If you consider online networking to be a core part of your professional development, you might choose to keep up with ten to twenty blogs. Personally, I have over twenty business analysis and project management blogs fed into my home page, and I know that this is merely a snapshot of what is being talked about online.

Set aside a time to check in on these sites regularly, set up alerts, or sign up for their RSS feeds. It does not matter how you choose to stay informed, only that you develop a method that works for you.

Advanced Online Networking

If you find that you would like to do even more to increase your online professional presence, below are a few more ideas to up your game:

- **Write a blog.** If you have a lot to say and want an independent platform to share your experiences, consider authoring your own blog. You should be prepared to post one or two times per week. Setting up a blog is also a fine way to stay informed about or gain exposure to the basics of web technology.
- **Guest post on other websites.** Writing articles for other websites is a viable alternative if you do not want to post at least once or twice per week but would still like to publish your professional thinking. Many websites host guest posts as a way to keep their content fresh and their publication pipeline full. Some social media sites also host blogs as well, specifically http://www.modernanalyst.com and http://www.batimes.com.
- **Become a power networker on LinkedIn.** Every person you are connected with on LinkedIn opens up your LinkedIn profile to more people, increasing the chances that you will show up in

other people's search results. Use the search function to find relevant connections, and personalize your connection requests for a better response rate.

How To Keep Up The Momentum

A common pitfall of networking is to meet a number of new people and then lose touch with them over time. Establishing the initial connection is the most difficult aspect of networking. Given this, you would do well to find a way to stay in touch with the people you meet and build on those relationships.

As you develop professionally, you will probably find yourself in a position to share something with someone you have met or learn something new from them.

How you stay in contact is a matter of personal preference, and you might choose different methods for different people. Below are some ideas:

- Send thank you cards to all your informational interviewees. This is a nice and unexpected touch that reminds them of your conversation.
- Let your new contacts know about the progress you are making toward your business analysis career goals, whether that be training, experience, a new job, or a promotion. You can choose to send out regular e-mails, update your online professional profiles, share your successes using status updates summarizing what you have learned or what you have been up to, or choose all of the above. Let them help you celebrate your success.
- Persist in paying it forward by sending useful information. Harness what you have learned about what your new contacts need. Even consider doing a little independent research and forwarding it along.

- Seek out people you have met with the next time you see them at a meeting. Say hello, and check in on how things are going.
- Contact specific individuals about openings in their domain or organization, and ask for input.

Staying in contact over the long term will trigger your contacts' memories about you and your career change if a position opens up.

A Final Word About Networking

In-person and online networking can be a consuming and sometimes distracting activity. It is important that you set personal goals for what you want to achieve through networking and regularly assess your progress toward these goals.

Consider whether you are learning what you set out to learn, if you are meeting relevant connections and finding new opportunities. Challenge yourself to ask better questions and do what it takes to build real connections.

✓ Putting It To Practice #16

Update Your Networking Plan

The tasks included in this chapter are intended to give you an idea of the types of professional networking activities that are valuable for new business analysts. After a month or two of exploring online resources, attending networking events, and conducting informational interviews, re-visit this chapter with a fresh perspective. Evaluate the results you have achieved against the goals you laid out in the beginning.

- What activities provided the most benefit?
- Where could you improve upon how you interact with others?
- What have you learned?
- What fresh perspectives did you find?
- Are you meeting your networking goals?

Invest more time where you are seeing the most results. For example, if you are meeting relevant connections at your local IIBA chapter, consider volunteering at a future meeting.

Stop doing any activities that are not adding value. For example, after conducting a handful of informational interviews, you might not be learning much new information. This could be the right time to switch to the strategy of asking individual questions.

As you grow professionally, the activities you find value in will change. Review your in-person and online networking plans periodically. Adjust your activities based on your goals and where you are receiving the most benefit.

CHAPTER

5

Focus On The Right Business Analyst Role For You

I became a business analyst when I no longer saw technology as the only solution.

~ Steve Blais

In this chapter we will explore common types of business analyst roles and help you determine which type of position will be the best fit with your skill set, circumstances, and career goals.

Business analyst jobs come in many different flavors. While it can be tempting to yearn for a world in which one definition of what a business analyst does prevails and, therefore, you are hypothetically qualified for every business analyst position, business analysts exist to add value to organizations. Each organization will define a business analyst role that yields maximum value.

While it might seem counter-intuitive, the variation among roles within the profession can be a huge benefit to you as a new business analyst. Your special skills and areas of expertise can be immensely valuable in securing your first or next business assignment while you build toward your longer-term career goals.

In this chapter, we will review some of the common types of business analyst roles and then help you figure out in what direction you want to head. But first, let's talk about a critical concept that helps define business analyst roles: the business-technology balance.

The Business-Technology Balance

While our profession is called *business analysis*, the vast majority of business analyst roles as they exist today deal specifically with software projects. Business change and software implementations tend to go hand-in-hand. Even so, some roles focus more on aligning the business team around the scope of a solution, and some focus more on detailed requirements for the technical team to implement.

Although the business analyst characteristically reports up to a manager either on the business team or on the technology team, a business analyst conceptually sits between the two. On the business side are the efforts to collaborate with business stakeholders and subject matter experts to understand the problem they need solved, map their business process, and help them align around what a profitable solution entails. On the technology side is working with the implementation team to define the solution within project constraints, detail functional software requirements, and resolve project issues.

It is doubtful that any position maintains an exact balance, and multiple characteristics impact the scope of any given business analyst role. If you have multiple stakeholders, especially more than three or four, you will probably spend more time working through business problems and aligning stakeholders around the scope of the solution. If you have a lesser number of stakeholders or someone else takes care of managing stakeholder input, such as a product manager, you might spend more time working on the system side and incorporating the requirements into an existing system. When a strong architect or application development lead oversees the implementation team, he or she might be content with a strong set of business requirements and be able to work through the functional specifications with you serving as the stakeholder.

In a business-focused role, you might have the following responsibilities:

- Understanding the needs of multiple stakeholders.
- Facilitating the negotiation of requirements amongst multiple stakeholders.
- Identifying the current- and future-state business processes.
- Helping the business stakeholders envision the future and how their work will need to change to support the future.

In a technology-focused role, you might have the following responsibilities:

- Creating, analyzing, and validating detailed functional specifications.
- Facilitating design sessions with the implementation team to define the solution.
- Delivering elements of systems design, including data migration rules, business rules, wireframes, or other detailed deliverables.

Below are some questions to consider as you determine where you would like to land on the business-technology balance:

- Do you want to be more immersed with the business side, helping facilitate consensus and solve business problems?
- Do you want to work from a fairly defined set of business goals or objectives and facilitate the solution?
- Do you enjoy elicitation more than analysis (or vice versa)?

No matter how a business analysis role is defined, you will feel some pull from one side to the other as you help negotiate realistic solutions to business problems.

The Role Of The System Analyst

While it should be clear by now that business analyst roles adapt in their scope or focus, you might be wondering about roles with the title of *Business Systems Analyst* or *Systems Analyst*. Even when the word Systems is included in the job title, it does not mean that the role is technology-focused.

Within the business analysis profession, *job titles* diverge substantially from *job roles*. Titles are used with very little consistency. According to Kevin Brennan, Executive Vice President of Product Management & Development of IIBA, at least five definitions of the job title *Systems Analyst* are in use. In the comments on a Bridging the Gap article, he cited the following definitions:

1. A synonym for business analyst;
2. An IT-focused business analyst (in organizations that split the BA role into more than one specialist role);
3. A hybrid business analyst/developer;
4. A systems architect (with no responsibility for requirements);
5. Help desk support.[8]

Given this reality, when you are reviewing job postings or talking to other professionals and you hear the term Systems Analyst come up, it is worth investigating what it is the role actually entails and not make any assumptions.

The first definition is addressed throughout this entire chapter, as we are discussing the different types of business analyst jobs. The third definition will be discussed specifically in the section on hybrid business analysis roles. The fourth and fifth definitions are outside the scope of this book, as they are not business analysis roles at all.

---

[8] http://www.bridging-the-gap.com/difference-between-a-business-analyst-and-systems-analyst/

Next let's turn our attention to the second definition, which is by far one of the more common applications of the job title Systems Analyst.

Splitting Up The Business Analyst Function

Some organizations split the business analysis role into two separate job functions. The first one is generally a business-side business analyst, who focuses on the business aspects of the process. The person in this role is responsible for delivering business requirements.

The second one is generally a systems or requirements analyst, who is responsible for fleshing out the business requirements into functional specifications to be fulfilled by a system or set of systems. Sometimes multiple systems analysts are employed, one assigned to each system impacted by the project. The systems analyst may take on technical design responsibilities and, if so, more technical coding knowledge tends to be required.

The hand-off between the two can fluctuate. Sometimes it is split at business requirements, other times at functional requirements, and still other times both roles work together through the full requirements lifecycle but share responsibilities in other ways.

Alex Papworth held a systems analyst role similar to the one described above at one point in his career. As he characterized it, he was an IT business analyst who liaised with a business-side business analyst to understand the requirements. He found this role career-limiting because he was not permitted to elicit requirements from the business stakeholders. If he had questions for the business, the business analyst intermediated and took them back to the business on his behalf.

On the other hand, business systems analyst roles exist where the ability to fulfill the systems design responsibilities is viewed as a senior-level competency. I have met several business analysts and managers who reported that within their organizations, business analysts are promoted based on an advanced level of domain and systems-specific knowledge within their organization. In these organizations, systems knowledge is valued because it enables the business systems analyst to be more efficient in their analysis and anticipate impacts to integrated systems.

These roles tend to be more technical, and while qualified individuals may not be software developers, they do have a well-developed understanding of the assorted technical implementation options available to help drive informed decisions around systems design. It follows that, in some organizations, a comprehensive understanding of the company, systems, or industry is valued more than the underlying business analyst competencies. We will dig into some more specific examples of how expertise in an industry domain and systems application may impact roles in the next section.

When it comes to the business-technology balance, two key points need to be underscored.

1. From the perspective of *business analysis* as a profession, no separate role called systems analyst exists, even though this term is frequently used as a job title.
2. As you progress through your *business analyst career*, consider if you want to develop systems knowledge as a part of your career progression. Extensive knowledge in a system or domain may be rewarded by advancement within your organization but tends not to be as transferable to other organizations as your core business analysis skills.

With these distinctions in mind, let's turn our attention to other types of specialized roles within business analysis.

Specializations Within Business Analysis

Beyond the balance of business and technology, many business analyst roles require special skills or focus on specific elements of the business analyst role. Many factors influence the make-up of a specific role. This section details the most common specializations found among business analyst positions.

Industry-Focused Business Analyst Roles

Some business analysis jobs focus on specific industries and require years of experience and in-depth familiarity with that industry. This is not all that different from other professions where knowledge of an industry may also be a requirement.

Industry experience enables a business analyst to understand the organizational context before ever speaking with a stakeholder. For some business analyst jobs, the business analyst fills the role of subject matter expert and analyst. This means that instead of eliciting all of the requirements from stakeholders, the business analyst is the source of many requirements. These roles require expertise in the industry as a job qualification.

Other business analyst roles simply prefer industry experience. Sometimes the hiring manager feels that their industry is too difficult to learn quickly. They would rather hire someone who already knows the essential industry terminology to shorten the time it takes for the analyst to be effective.

A lot of debate takes place as to whether industry expertise is particularly relevant to the business analysis profession, as a talented business analyst can get up to speed on knowledge areas fairly quickly and elicit business requirements regardless of their level of prior knowledge. Regardless of what side of the debate you find yourself on, in reality, many hiring managers show a strong preference for industry expertise.

Let's consider an example of how industry expertise may impact your business analysis career options. Durga Patil came into the business analyst role in the insurance industry with a technical background. After developing solid working relationships with her stakeholders, they advised her that to advance her career, she should pursue education to acquire domain knowledge in the insurance industry. She decided to pursue an academic degree in insurance, which taught her much of what she needed to know and helped her understand her customer's perspective. The rest of the domain knowledge she developed through her experience on many projects.

Similarly, Dave Schrenk, also from the insurance industry, pursued many certifications through the Insurance Institute of America. He found that they helped his career because the courses and certifications provided a wealth of knowledge related to the daily operations of an insurance company.

Adriana Beal took an alternate approach to break into the finance industry. "Before my first job as a business analyst for a financial institution on Wall Street, I worked for the equivalent in Brazil to the U.S. GAO (Government of Accountability Office) as an auditor. I'm sure my experience with public finance had a positive influence in the decision to hire me as a junior business analyst."[9]

Adriana recommends seeking out projects that help you build related experience when trying to break into a new industry.

It is probable that you bring expertise in one or more industries from the career experience you already have. Identify the companies for which you have worked throughout your career and consider what industries you have experience in.

Common industries requiring specific expertise from business analysts include:

---

[9] http://www.bridging-the-gap.com/help-a-ba-how-do-i-break-into-the-financial-industry-with-no-industry-experience/

- Finance
- Healthcare
- Insurance
- Logistics
- Oil and gas
- Real estate
- Telecommunications
- Travel

One way that you could delve into potential industries would be to go to LinkedIn and add a new role to your profile. LinkedIn provides a list of industries to select from, and this is a reasonable starting point for identifying your industry expertise. Most job boards also offer you the option to narrow your search by industry and provide a list from which to begin. At a comprehensive level, NAICS (North American Industry Classification System) codes are also used to classify organizations.[10] These codes provide a granular insight into potential industries that might be applicable for you.

Not all organizations fit neatly within one industry. For example, I worked for an online job board. In one respect, this organization was a technology company because we built and provided a technology-rich product. In another respect, this organization also fit into the professional recruiting industry because we were part of the employer's candidate search process. I can claim some expertise in both industries.

In addition to considering the industry of the company you have worked for, consider other industries you have been exposed to as part of your work. For example, one of my coaching clients was responsible for account set-up and support for between ten and twenty new businesses each month. He learned about their business processes

[10] For a complete list of NAICS codes: http://www.census.gov/eos/www/naics/ Accessed 10/9/2014.

and key requirements as they impacted his role in helping them get set up. In his case, some of his industry experience came not from the industry his company was in, but from the industry his customers were in. If you have specialized in helping customers within a certain industry, you might have relevant experience in that industry as well.

Below are some questions to consider before pursuing an industry-focused business analyst role:

- Do you have a passion for your current industry?
- Would you like to have experiences across multiple industries or build a professional expertise within a specific industry?
- Are you willing to invest the time (and possibly financial resources) necessary to build industry expertise?
- What will be the state of your chosen industry in five, ten, or twenty years?
- If your chosen industry declines and the job market no longer provides the right types of employment, are there parallel industries in which your knowledge and expertise will be similarly valued?

Functional Domain-Focused Business Analyst Roles

Expertise in a functional domain gives you insider knowledge about how the area inside the business works. Some business analyst teams are organized by functional area of the business. On these teams, each business analyst is assigned to one or more business units and works primarily with stakeholders from that business unit on projects that impact it. These business analysts develop expertise in the processes and systems used by their stakeholders.

To find your functional area expertise, consider the areas of the business you have worked in personally and the functional areas of any stakeholders you have worked with, either inside or outside your organization. For example, many standard accounting processes change little from one organization to another. If you have worked in accounting or worked on accounting projects, you have been exposed to accounting processes and have some level of accounting expertise. The same is true for sales, marketing, human resources, operations, information technology, and any other box you might find on an organizational chart.

Below are some questions to consider before pursuing a functional domain-focused business analyst role:

- Are you drawn to particular areas of the business? For example, are you excited by new product development, updated accounting regulations, or new human resource initiatives?
- Do you have experience in a specific functional domain across multiple organizations? Such experience helps you bring a broad perspective within a specific domain.
- Is your selected functional domain or department growing and evolving? Is there a stream of improvements you can help the business make?

Tool-Specific Business Analyst Roles

Some business analyst jobs require expertise in specific tools and technologies that are not part of the business analyst workflow but instead are part of the stakeholder workflow. Common examples include implementing complex applications, such as enterprise resource management, customer relationship management, and accounting systems.

When an organization has deployed a specific tool as part of its business processes, it can be valuable for the business analyst to understand the functionality and customization options that the tool offers. This knowledge helps the business analyst verify that the business stakeholders are fully leveraging the tool's capabilities to improve their processes. It can also help streamline the requirements analysis process.

After the initial deployment of the tool, most new projects will be focused on improving how the organization leverages the tool or customizing the tool to meet organizational needs. When the business analyst understands the tool, they can suggest requirements and solution approaches that are simpler and fit within the structure of the toolset in which the organization has already invested.

Some of these jobs require more technical know-how and involve configuring the tool for the organization, importing data, and supporting administrative activities. These roles are found most often within consulting companies, as few organizations find it necessary to hire someone with this kind of expertise on a full-time basis. However, bigger organizations might hire a tool expert in-house.

Below are some sample tools that a business analyst may be an expert in:

- Great Plains
- InfusionSoft
- Microsoft SharePoint
- QuickBooks
- Salesforce.com
- SAP (which stands for Systems, Applications, and Products in Data Processing)

Roles requiring expertise in a high-demand tool may be more lucrative than other business analyst roles simply because it may be difficult to find enough candidates with the required expertise. However, focusing on a specific area of expertise can also be risky. If the tool provider goes out of business or does something that causes a loss of customers, the value of your expertise could be short-lived.

Background experience as a user, subject matter expert, or implementer of an application may help you qualify for a business analyst position that requires specific tool or process expertise. To find out if your expertise is relevant in your local area, use the product names in job search engines and see what types of roles you find. Tool-specific business analyst jobs may be titled something other than *business analyst*, with *project manager* or *implementation engineer* being common examples. These are generally found to be hybrid roles, which are discussed a bit later.

Any tools you have used as an end user or analyzed as a business analyst are part of the functional application expertise that you bring to the table. To find more qualifications in this area, you might also be able to generalize expertise working with custom software so that it is relevant to other organizations. Many organizations use proprietary tools or systems. A proprietary system is a custom-built technology application designed specifically to support an organization's business and information management processes.

For example, one organization I worked for had a tool that it called The GUI, which provided customer management capabilities. There is a funny story behind this nickname. When the tool was deployed, it replaced the original phone-based customer management system. Graphical user interfaces (or GUIs), which are the visual ways we interact with a computer system using windows, icons, and menus, have become ubiquitous today. At the time, most of the people within the organization had never heard the term. As a result, the technical acronym GUI stuck as the way to refer to this computer system.

Even though The GUI was a custom software application, it was a type of sales automation and customer management tool. Understanding The GUI constituted experience with these types of software applications.

Below are some questions to consider before pursuing a tool-focused business analyst role:

- Would expertise in a specific application or tool elevate your role within your organization?
- Would expertise in a specific application or tool make you more marketable for a broad range of jobs in which you are interested?
- Do you want to see tangible outcomes from your efforts, such as improvements to a business process or customization of a tool to meet a user's specific needs?

Before we move on from this area of expertise, let's evaluate one more example from my career that might help you view the trajectory of your own career experiences and accumulated expertise in assorted industries, functional areas, and functional applications.

I spent the early part of my career focused in the publishing industry working on online content products for libraries. We digitized print content, put it online, and made it search-friendly and accessible so library patrons could browse the encyclopedia content online.

Before I moved to the online job board company, I saw myself as someone who had an expertise in online publishing products. But once I moved to the job board, I learned that there were a lot of similarities between publishing jobs and resumes online and publishing encyclopedia content online. The main difference was that jobs and resumes involved user-generated or customer-generated content. My prior experience was relevant, but I also broadened my perspective in my new role. I transitioned from having an expertise in publishing products to having an expertise in content-rich web applications.

I made a jump from end user applications to business-to-business applications when I secured a contract to help design a customer portal for builders in the building insurance industry, a completely new domain for me. However, one of the reasons I was hired was because I had experience designing customer-facing web systems.

Then I became involved in social media and blogging at Bridging the Gap, taking the expertise I had and applying it to use tools like Twitter, LinkedIn, and WordPress as part of building my own business. Later I was able to secure business analyst contracts for companies as diverse as a social media website for disabled persons, a community newspaper conglomerate wanting to improve its online presence, and a wedding website.

As you assess your own career trajectory, pay attention to the industries in which you have worked or helped, the functional areas in which you have worked, and the tools with which you have worked or have improved. You will find areas of expertise and experience you can use to help you forge paths within business analysis and ease your path of career development.

However, industry, functional domain, and business tools are not the only specialized areas of expertise relevant to business analysts. Let's look at some other types of specialized business analyst roles.

Business Intelligence Analysts

A growing field within information technology is business intelligence. Business intelligence projects support the strategic direction of an organization by enabling it to proactively mine information to make better decisions.

In their infancy, such projects were primarily the domain of those with knowledge and experience in data modeling and the commercial business intelligence tools available to an organization. But as the basics of business intelligence are put in place, organizations often realize that turning data into intelligence requires an understanding of the business processes through which data is generated. As such, this is becoming an increasingly viable career path for the business analyst with a strong background in data-intensive work who can also analyze processes and communicate with business stakeholders.

Below are some questions to consider before pursuing a specialty as a business intelligence analyst:

- Do you enjoy working with data?
- Are you familiar with tools for managing data? Can you use basic SQL (structured query language) commands to manipulate and report on data? Would you consider yourself an expert in Microsoft Excel?
- Do you have experience working with any specific data warehousing or business intelligence tools as an end user or developer?
- Do you enjoy posing difficult questions and finding creative ways that data can help your organization answer those questions?
- Are you interested in developing and maintaining technical expertise?

Business Process Analyst

Business changes happen all the time, and with business change comes business process change. Let's consider just a few of many possible examples:

- New departments are formed to respond to regulatory requirements or support new products and services.
- An organization decides to invest in changing how it does business in order to optimize organizational efficiencies or deliver increased customer satisfaction.
- An organization faces a customer retention problem and appoints a task force to investigate the problem and recommend solutions.

All of these scenarios involve changes that have scope, requirements, and lots of moving parts. They may involve supporting application changes too, but they are not centered around the development of a new application.

A business process analyst, or business analyst with a process focus, leads the efforts to identify business process problems, finds ways to improve existing business processes, and implements the resulting business process changes. Many of the tools and techniques used by technology-focused analysts are directly applicable to the process-focused analyst.

Business process analyst roles may also involve designing new processes from the ground up. Alex Papworth, a freelance business analyst, took on a just such a project. His client needed to change all of its client contracts and gain agreement from its customers to meet a new legal requirement. The project's first phase involved analyzing client contracts to determine the changes and communicate those changes to the client base. The second phase required the establishment of a call center to deal with queries and an operational process to validate returned signed contracts.

Alex designed an operating model to support processing queries and documents. Subsequently, new, temporary teams were formed to support the operating model. The operating model included business processes and defined service level agreements and a team structure.

Alex reports that as a business process analyst, you have to be sensitive to the fact that people will be executing the process. People can generate errors that you need to handle in your process, but they also want to be treated with respect.

A key difference between a business process analyst role and a business-focused business analyst on a technology project is that a business process analyst is likely to be involved in working with people to see the changes through to the end. Instead of technology implementing a solution, the business itself implements the solution. The project is complete when the improvement or change has become part of the organization's normal day-to-day operation. After project completion, the business process analyst may be involved in monitoring the success of the change, measuring the return on investment, and suggesting new changes that are now possible given the current state of the business operating system.

As the business analysis profession matures and technology solutions become even easier to implement, it is expected that we will see roles that are less wrapped around technology solutions and more wrapped around business problems. Business process modeling is one way that the business analyst can come to a clear understanding of the problem to be solved, and many business analysts see it as a step up if they can move away from technology solutions and into the business problem space.

Below are some questions to consider before pursuing a business process analyst role:

- Is your passion for business analysis at all tied to seeing new systems up and running? Would you enjoy identifying solutions that have little to no technology component?
- Are you prepared to fully challenge people to make the necessary changes to implement new improvements?
- Are you ready to apply your analysis and critical thinking skills to a collection of people, processes, and systems?

Product Business Analysts

Some business analyst roles are involved in creating customer-facing software products, including web-based applications and downloadable software applications. On these projects, your primary stakeholders come from the product and marketing groups. In this role, the business analyst might also help bridge the gap between the product/marketing group and the internal processes needed to support the product in customer service or accounting. Sometimes a separate business analyst group or stakeholder holds this responsibility.

While business analysts in these types of jobs might have external customer interaction, the amount of direct interaction with users of the system may be much more limited than when working with internal business stakeholders. As a result, working on a product may feel more like a hypothetical journey. While occasions present themselves for acquiring direct end user feedback, they are fewer and come in the form of focus groups, beta tests, usability tests, and demos. Sometimes the product or marketing manager owns this communication loop, but frequently business analysts are involved, at least as observers.

Below are some questions to consider before pursuing a product business analyst specialization:

- Are you willing to take this hypothetical journey with your product and marketing team concerning what the customer wants?
- Are you willing to re-work your product concepts and requirements based on customer feedback?
- Does the idea of building something new that fills a need that your users might not even fully understand yet excite you?
- Do you like working with innovative people who are focused on achieving big visions?

The Common Thread

A common thread emerges from these specializations. The business analyst is responsible for solving a business problem. Steve Blais has been in what we now call the business analysis profession for forty years. He described his transition from a programmer/systems analyst to a business analyst:

> "Like most business analysts at the time, it happened quite by accident. I was a programmer, then a programmer analyst. People kept asking me to talk to the business. This probably happened because I was a good listener. I started doing what we now define as business analysis.
>
> First, as a systems analyst I was originally focused on systems design. Over time, my roles became less focused on the systems aspect of the solution and more focused on the business aspect.
>
> From a career perspective, I decided I did not want to spend my life on the marketability treadmill of keeping up with the latest technology trend. The problems of business are often new, but you don't need technology to solve them. You need common sense and knowledge of people.
>
> **I became a business analyst when I no longer saw technology as the only solution."**[11]

Whether you are focused on business process solutions, developing new software, or implementing off-the-shelf software, you are fulfilling the mission of a business analyst. Most of the specializations we have stepped through are wrapped around the type of solutions that we provide to solve business problems. When you can step away from a specific way of solving a problem and help discover the best possible solution, then you have landed yourself firmly in the business analyst profession.

While it would be nice if the business analysis profession was only organized around areas of specialization, the roles available to you have an additional layer of complication in that it is not uncommon to find roles that combine business analysis responsibilities

---

[11] http://www.bridging-the-gap.com/essence-business-analysis-steve-blais/

with responsibilities from other professions. In the next section, we will survey hybrid business analyst roles.

Hybrid Business Analyst Roles

Many organizations, intentionally or not, blend the business analysis role with another role in the organization. This trend could become more common as different methodologies switch up the make-up of traditional technology and process improvement teams.

Hybrid roles come with their own challenges. While splitting the role apart may preclude individuals from experiencing all aspects of a profession, hybrid roles risk spreading individuals too thinly and may keep them from rising within any given profession.

However, because business analysis work tends to ebb and flow, hybrid roles can keep you busy during down times. At the beginning of a project, you might be overwhelmed with activities, but during active development or toward the end of your activities and project, involvement may wane. Being able to take on responsibilities from related roles means that you are more liable to stay busy and be a consistent contributor.

This section details some of the more common hybrid roles filled by business analysts.

Project Manager / Business Analyst

On the best of teams, project management and business analysis responsibilities go hand-in-hand, and the line between the two is gray. Combining the two roles into one person means that in addition to your business analysis responsibilities, you will be accountable for scope, schedule, cost, and managing the implementation through deployment. This is a common blend even in bigger organizations that simply choose not to separate the two roles. If you wish to transition from a project manager into a business analyst role, these blends will enable you to grow your business analysis experience, and you will tend to be well-qualified for the positions.

Project management roles may involve the following types of responsibilities:

- Project planning/scheduling
- Estimation
- Status reporting
- Project communication
- Portfolio management

Kym Byron, CBAP and PMP, has held a combined role and enjoyed it. She found that it gave her ownership of the project. With a combined role, it is not just about writing the requirements and letting everyone else figure it out. By taking on project management responsibilities, the business analyst gets to see her requirements through to the end solution and implementation.

Indeed, the role can be fulfilling and provide a career path for project managers or business analysts hoping to transition from one career to the other. It can also help professionals from either role build new skills and accumulate experiences that might qualify them for management positions in the future.

Many business analysts see project management as the next step in their career. However, many business analysts do not want to be project managers or have tried the project management route only to find that it does not fit their skills and competencies.

Trust that to advance your career, you do not have to switch professions. Business analysis provides countless career options as you develop into a senior-level professional.

Below are some questions to consider if you find yourself in a hybrid project manager / business analyst role:

- What do you like about the role?

- Do you naturally lean more toward business analysis or project management?
- What competencies from the business analyst profession do you rely on most?
- What competencies from the project management profession do you rely on most?
- What are your weak spots from the perspective of each profession?

Below are some questions to consider before pursuing a hybrid project manager / business analyst role:

- Do you see either business analysis or project management as the more senior-level role?
- How will taking on a hybrid role move your career forward?
- Do you have the diligence it takes to swap hats so that you can effectively manage both aspects of your role?
- What project management skills do you need to build to be successful?
- What business analysis skills do you need to build to be successful?

Business Analyst / Quality Assurance Engineer

The hybrid business analyst and quality assurance role is another common blend founded on the premise that those who defined the requirements are in the best position to test against the requirements. This assumption can be valid, especially in smaller organizations.

Both functions share a common value: a drive for high-quality software. And when one role is vacant, people in the complementary role tend to fill the gap. I have seen skillful testers become business analysts because no one was defining requirements, and therefore, they did not have any specifications to test against. I have also seen committed business analysts test simply because they were driven to see their requirements through to completion.

Quality assurance roles may involve the following responsibilities:

- Test planning
- Manual software testing
- Automated testing
- Performance testing
- User acceptance testing
- Process audits

The hybrid business analyst / quality assurance engineer role tends to work best for projects that do not involve formal quality engineering, such as test automation and performance testing. The combined role can make sense for projects that are chiefly implementing off-the-shelf products, since these technology solutions have already been functionally tested. In a combined role, it is not uncommon for the business analyst to focus on coordinating user acceptance testing by the business subject matter experts rather than building and executing a full-fledged test plan.

This hybrid role can also be useful on shorter projects or in organizations with few technology staff. For example, on a team with three or fewer developers who are focused on minor changes to an existing software system, one person may be able to fill both roles without being stretched too thin. They may also take on some project management and coordination tasks.

As a business analysis professional with quality assurance responsibilities, recognize that these added activities could eventually hold you back from more senior-level business analysis roles. The deadline-driven nature of most quality assurance efforts might preclude you from being involved in projects early enough to participate fully in discussions about scope, return on investment, and business needs. The opposite would be true for a quality assurance professional, where upfront accountabilities to identify requirements may preclude an individual from the full deployment of concerns within the quality assurance discipline or taking time to learn senior-level quality assurance duties, such as how to use automation tools to run tests.

Below are some questions to consider before pursuing a hybrid business analyst / quality assurance engineer role:

- Do you have a passion to see your project through to completion?
- Do you have the detail orientation required to fully test all system functionality and confirm the overall quality of the system?
- Do you like the idea of working on a smaller team or organization and wearing multiple hats?
- Could you foresee yourself transitioning from a combined business analyst / quality assurance *contributor* to a business analyst / quality assurance lead or *manager*? Experience in both professions could prepare you to lead a team of business analysts and quality assurance professionals.

Developer / Programmer Analyst

Combined developer / programmer analyst roles involve requirements analysis and the development of working software. It is not uncommon for developers to work directly with end users of internal software, subject matter experts, or product managers. In these situations, the role of the business analyst may be split, with the business-side stakeholder taking some ownership of what a business analyst would call business requirements and needs and the developer taking ownership of technical specifications and requirements validation. Often, the requirements process may be fairly informal, if defined at all, and the focus is on collaborative communication to generate working software.

In general, developer roles may include the following responsibilities:

- Systems design
- Technical design
- Programming/coding
- Database development
- Unit testing

Hybrid software developer and programmer analyst roles are common in companies with informal development practices. Business analyst roles may emerge from these organizations as the software development team grows and roles need to be differentiated in order to scale the team. These types of hybrid roles are also common in web development shops, where technology developments tend to be more design- and user-centered, and in circumstances where the developers have an abundance of business domain knowledge.

Like the other hybrid roles discussed above, the developer / programmer analyst role will pull you in multiple directions and eventually will become a stopping point in your career development unless you choose to build your expertise in one area or the other. If you are able to excel in both aspects of the role and want to maintain your technical expertise in programming and software development, you may have an aptitude for enterprise architecture or leadership roles in the development team.

Below are some questions to consider before pursuing a hybrid developer / programmer analyst role:

- As a developer, can you maintain a level of abstraction about what problem you are solving? Can you think independently about what is needed before you consider how you will implement it?
- If you had to choose between your development role and your analyst role, which would you choose?
- What aspects of development do you enjoy most? How can you structure a role in which you do more of that work?

Product Manager

Product managers own the concept for a product that the organization sells. A product manager may be the hub of product-related activities within an organization, from sales training, marketing, and building or upgrading the product functionality.

Product manager responsibilities may include:

- Identifying ideas for new products
- Identifying product enhancement ideas
- Being a liaison for key customers
- Training sales staff
- Developing marketing plans
- Researching the competition
- Completing budget and sales forecasts

The product manager who also performs business analysis responsibilities might take on tasks such as defining business requirements or liaising with the technical team about product specifications as well. In organizations with both business analysis and product management roles, the product manager is typically the primary business stakeholder for new product developments and consolidates input from a number of sources (customers, customer service, marketing, sales, web research, and competitive analysis, among others) into a concept for a new product or product enhancement.

Regardless of whether the product manager is responsible for the detailed requirements and communication with the technical team about the requirements, a product manager holds many responsibilities related to defining the business need, problem, and opportunity. For example, a product manager may research and author a business case to justify new investments, conduct a return on investment analysis, and define a clear customer need to support further elicitation of requirements.

Product manager positions tend to require specific industry experience. For a product-focused business analyst, the product manager role might seem like the only next step up within their organization. Many business analysts struggle with whether to invest in building their business analyst competencies or focus on domain-specific knowledge that will make them promotable into product roles within their organization.

Below are some questions to consider before you consider pursuing a product manager role:

- Are you ready to own the product?
- Does the idea of envisioning a solution to a customer problem ignite your passions?
- Would you be prepared to let go of some of the more detailed requirements for your solution so that you can stay focused on the big picture of the product and all of the related activities that go with launching a product?
- Are you prepared to maintain the product, which might involve supporting sales people, calls with clients, forecasting revenue numbers, and prioritizing ongoing enhancements?

Product Owner

The product owner is a role on an agile software development team. The product owner is the main point of contact with the technical team about business priorities and the scope of business requests. They build and prioritize the product backlog and define the details of user stories. They are also responsible for accepting the work that the team completes during the course of sprints, or two to four week blocks of development effort.

The product owner may or may not be a product manager. The scope of the product owner's responsibilities might be for a customer-facing product, an internal business application, or a combination of the two.

To fulfill these responsibilities, the product owner must collaborate with stakeholders throughout the business who have a stake in the system(s) in question, understand the direction of the organization and how that impacts their product or system, understand the current capabilities of the system, and understand how the system supports the business.

In organizations with many integrated systems or multiple stakeholder groups, the product owner is sometimes supported by a team, which may include a business analyst, user interface designer, and tester(s).

A product owner role may provide an avenue for career growth and a way for a business analyst to increase the scope of their responsibilities, particularly when it comes to influencing the outcome of projects and decision-making. It might also be the only career path laid out for business analysts in organizations transitioning to a more agile software development process.

Below are some questions to ask yourself before pursuing a product owner role:

- Are you comfortable with the idea of being the single point of contact for everything the business wants or needs out of a software release?
- Do you like collaborating with the technical team about the solution?
- Are you prepared to test and provide ongoing feedback within the development cycle?
- Do you have a keen sense of how to prioritize requests?
- Are you willing to consider project dependencies alongside business needs to develop a usefully-ranked product backlog?

Information Architect

Many consulting firms helping companies design content-rich websites and software employ Information Architects (IAs) as part of the design process. IAs may also be employed full-time within organizations that have a lot of content to manage for internal business users and/or external partners and customers. Many of the information architecture roles include business analyst responsibilities as well. Common projects include websites, intranets, online communities, content management systems, and mobile applications.

Common job responsibilities of the information architect include:

- Content strategy
- Information model development
- Navigation mapping
- Taxonomy development
- User interface design
- Website navigation design

- Writing
- Usability testing and consulting

Information architecture positions may vary in their focus, some emphasizing how the content is organized and some emphasizing functional aspects of the user experience and usability. The scope of the information architecture responsibilities frequently includes working with a business sponsor to understand the business goals of the project and identify information architectures as part of the solution and serving as the liaison to the development team, whether through formal requirements or some other form of communication and specification. As the emphasis on usable software grows, this role will likely become a prominent one within many organizations.

The information architecture role is more solution- and design-oriented than a traditional business analyst role. While the information architect is still focused on fulfilling a business need and may collaborate with business stakeholders, they are much more apt to dig deep into how to solve that business need and be expected to have opinions about how to design the system from a visual and interactive perspective. As a business analyst, you might also work collaboratively with an information architect on a project where usability and content design are extremely important.

Several roles and titles encompass the types of responsibilities outlined above. Some of the more common titles are:

- User experience designer
- User interface designer
- User interaction designer
- Usability specialist/consultant/architect
- Content librarian
- Content strategist

- Web content manager
- Search engine optimizer

Below are some questions to consider before pursuing an information architect role:

- Do you have a keen eye for usability and user interaction?
- Are you interested in designing the solution?
- Are you willing to own and advocate for a specific design within the context of a project or product?
- Do you find yourself exploring content requirements and finding better ways to use content in your business or applications?

A Final Note About Hybrid Job Roles

No absolute right and wrong decisions exist when it comes to hybrid job roles. As you progress within the business analysis profession, you may find yourself building skills and competencies within several related roles. All of these skills can have a positive impact on your career prospects and your ability to progress within the business analysis profession.

However, if your goal is to grow your business analysis skill set, a hybrid job role may present specific challenges. We have a tendency toward the familiar. If you enter into a hybrid role with a strong background in the non-business analysis skill set, you will be likely to leverage your prior experience instead of truly learning the business analysis ropes.

In many organizations today, roles and responsibilities are shifting between teams and positions. This is especially true in organizations employing agile processes. These ways of building software throw most of the traditional roles out the window, leaving room for individuals to craft new roles or customize roles to suit their strengths and career goals. Finding the right position and starting your business analysis career is more about what you are doing to gain experience than what your title is.

Alternative Types Of Employment

Not all business analysts are employed in full-time jobs. The type of business analyst employment you choose may impact the role drastically. In this section, we'll delve into business analyst consultants, independent business analyst consulting, and contracting as a business analyst. These types of employment may include any of the specializations or hybrids discussed above.

Business Analyst Consultants

Companies may hire business analyst consultants for all kinds of projects, whether it be to re-design a process or a process area, develop proprietary software, or implement a new software application. Most often, business analyst consultants are hired as part of a consulting team that provides a comprehensive solution for the client. Less frequently, an organization offers business analysis as a stand-alone service. A consulting project may be called a client engagement.

As a business analyst within a consulting company, your time will be billed hourly to a client, and you may be required to be onsite at the client's office. This could require travel, which may be up to 100 percent of your time in some positions. Alternatively, a selected number of boutique consulting companies offer services in major cities where you may work predominately in local offices.

Business analyst consulting positions come in two primary designations. First, there are senior-level positions for project leaders that require several years of experience along with any specialized expertise required for the engagement. Second, select junior-level positions exist in large consulting organizations where business analysts follow a prescriptive process and mainly handle detailed analysis work. Consulting organizations are well known for hiring recent college graduates at entry-level salaries for these positions.

As a Deloitte consultant for several years, Adam Feldman reports that consulting requires you to be able to learn a new business quickly and help the client's stakeholders through the requirements methodology. As a consultant you might be dealing with sponsors and stakeholders who are put in situations in which a lot of change takes place, and it is necessary for you to cultivate a trusting relationship and educate the client-side stakeholders about the business process improvement and software development processes.

Below are some questions to consider before pursuing a business analyst role in a consulting company:

- Are you interested in learning about new organizations and building trust with new stakeholders with every client engagement?
- Are you willing to travel 50 to 100 percent of the time?
- Are you qualified for a senior-level position at a consulting company? Or are you a recent college graduate prepared to accept an entry-level role?

Independent Business Analyst Consultants

As an independent business analyst consultant, you take on short-term client engagements, frequently on a part-time basis, to serve specific business needs for your clients. High-level assignments could include helping an organization build a strategic plan, heading the development of a new technology strategy, or scoping a new project or product. You could also fill more tactical business analyst roles, such as defining the requirements for a specific undertaking.

Many independent consultants develop proprietary processes that they use to help clients in a particular niche or with a particular type of task. For example, Susan Penny Brown, Principal Consultant at Interim Technical Management, Inc., helps organizations align their information technology strategy with their business objectives and select enterprise applications that deliver strategic, competitive advantage. Susan uses a proprietary process to define business value, goals, and processes. She then discovers acceptable vendors, assesses their technology as well as their capacity to be a business partner, and negotiates the final agreement.

As an independent consultant, you are not only responsible for your client work, but you own a business and so are also responsible for operating the business, which involves everything from sales and marketing to accounting. Independent consultants spend a lot of time networking to find new clients and regularly find it necessary to sell the value of business analysis alongside selling their own professional abilities.

Below are some questions to consider before starting out as an independent business analyst consultant:

- Are you willing to learn how to build, grow, and run a business? Beyond business analysis, your responsibilities as an independent consultant will include marketing, sales, and accounting.
- Are you willing to invest a considerable amount of time building your network and developing your marketing and sales skills so that you can eventually have a steady stream of new clients?
- Are you qualified to specialize in any on-demand niches where you can command a premium rate for your work?

Contract Business Analysts

Contract work involves a full-time, short-term commitment to a specific organization, primarily to support the analysis effort for a specific project. The company hiring a contractor may need certain expertise for a short period of time or, for some other reason, cannot or will not commit to a full-time hire.

Contracting agreements may last anywhere from three months to upwards of two years in duration. It is not unusual for an organization to extend a short contract when a project takes longer than expected or when a proven contractor gets assigned to new projects. Many companies use contract-to-hire arrangements to trial a candidate before making a full-time hire or to work around budget constraints that prevent hiring a new employee.

When contracting, you will build new business analysis experiences, learn about a new organization, and extend your professional network. Even if the position is not specified as a contract-to-hire agreement, if you prove yourself, you could be top on the list should a full-time position open up. Some business analysts prefer to contract because of the higher hourly rates and relative amount of flexibility that contract work provides.

Contracting has its downsides as well. As a contractor on a team of full-time employees, you may not be involved in team meetings and other company events. You may not have as much access to mentoring assistance and training budgets.

While contracting positions do offer higher hourly rates, the higher rate does not necessarily mean higher take-home pay. Be sure to factor in the additional taxes and lack of benefits out of the higher hourly rate to make a fair comparison. And do not neglect any investments you will make in your own professional development.

As a contractor, it is also important to realize that you build your own career progression. The contracts you choose will dictate your career experiences and future career opportunities. You will need to strike a balance between being steadily employed and accepting contracts that do not make the most of your skills and competencies. In busier times, you will be able to pick and choose the best contracts and command higher rates. In slow times, you may need to accept a less desirable project at a lower rate to fill an income gap.

Below are some questions to consider before pursuing a business analyst contract position:

- Are you interested in learning about new organizations and building trust with new stakeholders with every new contract?
- Are you willing to take the risk of being temporarily out of work between contracts?
- Are you willing to take responsibility for your own career progression and professional development expenses?

Finding The Right Type Of Employment For You

Working in a consulting company, as an independent consultant, or as a contract business analyst all have their pros and cons when stacked up against full-time employment. You can build a fulfilling business analysis career in any of these situations or by mixing and matching them.

It is not uncommon for business analysts to contract independently for a while and then find a company they really like or a position that they are excited about and take a full-time position. It is also not uncommon for business analysts to leave a full-time position to experience the variety of independent work.

What's more, independent consulting and contracting do not have to be mutually exclusive. When I was first starting my independent consulting business, I took on a few selected contracts that I found through local recruiters to fill income gaps.

As you consider what types of business analyst employment agreements you would like to pursue, focus on both the short-term experiences you can gain as well as the long-term trajectory of your career. Most importantly, do not feel that you have to make a decision now that will stick for the duration of your business analysis career. There will be many occasions to reconsider your decision as you gain more experiences.

Putting It To Practice #17

Map Out Your Business Analysis Career Goal

In the next chapter, we will walk through the options you have for moving from where you are to where you want to be. Before we take that step, it is important that you give some serious thought to where you want to get to on this career journey.

Setting a career goal is difficult because it involves choosing to pursue some options and excluding others, at least for the time being. Instead of moving right to setting a clear and concise goal, take some time to do some thinking while nothing is set in stone.

(Although I will let you in on a little secret: Nothing is ever set in stone. You can always change your career goals when those goals no longer represent where you want to be.)

Given what you have learned about the types of business analyst roles available, what might a business analyst role look like for you?

Below are some specific questions to consider:

- Do your career intentions lean more toward the business side of business analysis or the technology side of business analysis?
- What business analyst responsibilities do you want to take on?
- Are there any business analyst responsibilities you want to avoid or minimize?
- What areas of expertise do you bring, and how could these help you in a business analyst role?
- What roles with business analysis responsibilities exist within your current organization? How might you incorporate one or more of those roles into your business analyst career path?
- What hybrid roles would you consider? Why?
- What specialized roles would you consider? Why?
- What hybrid or specialized roles do you want to avoid? Why?
- Would you consider a contract position? Why or why not?
- What types of consulting positions would you be interested in?
- How frequently are you willing to travel?
- What are your salary expectations?
- What benefits do you want?

Write down the answers to these questions as well as any other details about where you want to be. In the next chapter, we will see how to get from where you are today to where you want to be in the future and what steps to take along the way.

CHAPTER 6

Your Career Transistion Strategy

As a business analyst, you are champion for facilitating the change in an organization. If you fear change or fear the possibility of confronting a career change, you may be in trouble.
~ Yamo, The BA Coach

No one path will land you in a business analysis career. As you sit here reading this book, you bring a unique set of qualifications to the table. Your career background, particular set of experiences, and current employment situation guarantees that some paths have rich potential while others will make it more difficult to gain traction.

While much of the advice you find about getting started as a business analyst amounts to one person telling you what worked for them, the advice you will find in this chapter is based on my work with hundreds of aspiring, new, and even experienced business analysts who each found their own path into the profession. In what follows, I will walk you through the options you have along with when and why each option may or may not make sense to you. As you read through these options, take note of ideas that would help you move toward the career goal you mapped out at the end of the previous chapter.

(A complementary resource for this chapter is the free Business Analyst Career Roadmap, which visually shows you how the paths work together to get you to where you want to go. You may download your copy at: http://www.bridging-the-gap.com/business-analysis-career-roadmap/)

But first, let's tackle a path that is repeatedly unnoticed and make sure that you are not already where you intend to be.

Are You Already A Business Analyst?

It is not uncommon for someone to get to this step in initiating their business analysis career and realize that the work to do is not so much of a transition as a discovery. Countless professionals have extensive business analysis experience without ever having held the business analyst job title or being aware that a profession exists to support them in their career.

Let's examine a business analyst's story that began in just this way. Aaron Whittenberger started his career in accounting and finance but was soon involved in technology projects. Since he liked working with computers, his manager asked him to help install a new system and lead the project. From that point forward, Aaron kept on working in software development and project management capacities. It was not until twenty years into his technology career, when he attended a Business Analyst Bootcamp, that he realized that he had been doing a lot of business analysis as well.

Aaron decided to focus his career going forward on business analysis while working as a consultant for a local application development organization. Then he was surprised to learn that he could qualify to sit for the CBAP® (Certified Business Analysis Professional™) exam. He continued to fill hybrid software development / project management / business analysis roles while focusing his career development within business analysis.[12]

Some important takeaways from this story include:

- Even if you were not aware that you were doing business analysis tasks at the time, you could still have meaningful business analysis experience.

[12] http://www.bridging-the-gap.com/it-consultant-to-business-analyst/

- You can grow your business analysis career while filling hybrid roles.
- Sitting for the CBAP® exam may be an option even if you are newly discovering the business analysis profession.

Awakening into business analysis is a perfectly valid way to begin your business analysis career. Doing so requires that you take some time to appreciate the business analysis experiences you have already had and that you see yourself as a business analyst. You may choose to pursue training, expand your business analysis experiences by maturing your organization's business analysis approach, and securing a promotion or title change to business analysis. At this point, you have started your business analysis career, and your growth will come from expanding the scope of your responsibilities and cultivating your business analysis skill set.

However, you may not yet feel confident in your business analysis abilities, or you may not have had the chance yet to accumulate noteworthy business analysis experiences while filling other job roles. In the next section, we will review three types of leaps forward that you may consider as part of your short-term or long-term career planning.

Three Leaps Forward

If you are not already a business analyst, you will eventually need to change job roles to make your career goal a reality. Changing roles can be explicit in that you are hired or promoted into a new job with a new title or implicit in that you begin taking on new job responsibilities and essentially morph your current role into a new role.

How can you make these leaps? Let's first explore the three different types of jobs you might consider on your business analyst career path.

Leap Into A Junior-Level Business Analyst Position

The first option to beginning a business analyst career is finding a junior-level business analyst position. A junior-level business analyst role typically requires knowledge of core business analysis practices but not necessarily experience applying the practices in a real-world setting. In such a role, you may support a senior business analyst as a member of a business analyst team or take on less substantial projects with direct mentoring support from a more experienced business analyst. You would probably be following a well-developed business analysis process and receive a lot of direct support.

While this might seem like an ideal path, few junior-level business analyst positions are available. In any local area, you may find a handful of organizations that hire junior-level business analysts. Most commonly, these organizations will be sizeable companies and consulting organizations.

What is more, junior-level business analyst positions are generally filled by recent college graduates at entry-level professional salaries. If you are a recent college graduate with a degree in a related field, focusing on the organizations hiring junior-level business analysts can be an ideal path into business analysis. If you are a more senior-level professional with career experience outside of business analysis, finding a junior-level role does not tend to be a productive path. Even if you are willing to take a salary cut to get into the business analyst profession, you may be perceived as over-qualified for junior-level business analyst positions.

Below are some steps to take when following this path:

- Obtain education in the foundations of business analysis.
- Prepare to demonstrate proficiency in the underlying business analysis core competencies.

- Research your local area for companies that hire entry-level or junior-level business analysts. Apply for positions.
- Secure internships with local organizations to gain valuable experience and potential connections to junior-level business analyst jobs.
- Obtain an undergraduate degree, as that is usually a prerequisite for even junior-level business analyst positions. Selecting a degree in business analysis or a related discipline may increase your chances of being hired.

If this idea does not apply to you, do not be discouraged. It is actually the least common path to becoming a business analyst. Next we view a role that is relevant for mid-career professionals.

Leap Into A Mid-Level Or Senior-Level Business Analyst Position

Another common path into business analysis is to get hired or promoted directly into a mid-level or senior-level business analysis position. While the definitions of mid-level and senior-level business analysis roles differ from one organization to another, it can be useful to categorize jobs available and your own qualifications separately.

Mid-level business analysts tend to have knowledge and experience in a broad set of business analysis skills that enables them to handle many types of projects independently. These projects might vary in size and complexity.

Senior business analysts are regularly perceived as experts and are the go-to people in their organization. A senior business analyst may mentor other business analysts or lead a business analyst team on a project, coordinating the work of other business analysts to deliver requirements for a large, complex project. Senior business analysts may take on many extra responsibilities that directly support critical project work or building the business analyst practice. In some organizations, senior-level business analyst roles are defined by either business or technical domain expertise as opposed to business analyst skill sets.

By leveraging your professional network and your underlying business analysis competencies, you may be hired directly into a mid-level or senior-level business analysis role. Alternatively, you could leverage your industry, functional domain, or tool-specific expertise for a specialized business analysis role or your experience in a related domain for a hybrid role.

No matter what type of business analyst role you move into, it is possible that the role will be a bit beyond your qualifications, or maybe well beyond your qualifications. When you move into a mid-level or senior-level role, you may receive support on your first few projects from a senior business analyst, or you may be thrown into the position with little guidance.

My path to business analysis involved getting hired into a mid-level role with support. As I mentioned earlier, I was hired from a quality assurance position into a business analysis position. During my first few months, I shadowed a senior business analyst and supported her on a few projects. While I was not in a role classified as junior, I was essentially being treated as a junior-level business analyst.

Three months into my new position, however, one of the biggest technology projects in my company's history landed in my lap. I was solely responsible for the business analysis planning and requirements analysis for the entire project, which ended up spanning nearly a year, requiring over thirty use cases, integrating four different systems, and solving some rather technically-involved issues.

As my experience shows, getting hired directly into a mid-level business analyst role is a common path for individuals that seek internal business analysis positions. Since you have prior knowledge of your organization and understand either the business domain and/or the technical domain, you will be able to rely on your existing knowledge to help lead you to succeed even as you build up your business analysis skills.

Moving directly into a mid-level or senior-level business analysis role, even with limited support, may be a real possibility for individuals with a fair amount of professional experience. Having at least five years of experience in a related professional discipline helps you develop the business acumen and underlying business analysis competencies, thereby increasing your chances of success.

Curtis Michelson took this leap as an independent business analysis consultant. While he had been doing information technology and usability consulting for years, he landed a new client engagement that required a more formal business analysis approach. Curtis hired me to help him hone his elicitation plan and review his preliminary scoping deliverables. Curtis went on to consult as a business analyst and help many more organizations make sound project decisions.

Still other new business analysts find themselves thrown into what is essentially a mid-level or senior-level role when their team takes on a more substantial project than it has historically taken on or an executive learns about business analysis and decides to build a practice. They find themselves in the right place at the right time and rise to the occasion. Many business analysts unconsciously took this path into business analysis and realized only later in their careers that they were filling a business analyst role.

Below are some steps to take when following this path:

- Develop a clear understanding of the underlying business analysis core competencies you bring to the table. Make sure that they are well-represented on your resume and that you can speak to them in a job interview.

- Develop a clear understanding of any special or related skills that well qualify you for specific types of business analyst job roles. Again, highlight these skills on your resume, and focus on finding positions preferring them.
- Explore business analysis positions in your existing organization, recognizing that these jobs may or may not have the job title of business analyst.
- Invest in expanding your connections to business analysts and professionals that hire business analysts, internally and/or externally. Even if you do not bring specific business analysis skills that are required for the position, when someone has a first-hand impression of your ability to do similar work, they may be more inclined to hire you into a business analysis position.
- Invest in basic training in the fundamentals of business analysis. Such training will help you talk the talk as well as increase your confidence in your ability to fill the role.
- Build a support network that you can call on to get your questions answered and talk through important project challenges. This team could include internal business analysts and project managers, trusted external experts, and even a coach or mentor.
- Keep your eyes open for projects that would benefit from business analysis. Jump into these projects in any way you can.

If junior-level, mid-level, or senior-level roles are not suitable options for you, consider pursuing a transitional role. Let's talk about that next.

Leap Into A Transitional Role

On your journey to business analysis, you do not have to move directly into a business analysis role. Many successful business analysts consciously choose to pursue what is called a transitional role or an occupation that puts them in a position to do business analysis tasks or interact with business analysts. The role may or may not be formally assigned selected business analyst responsibilities.

Below are some situations in which a transitional role may represent a satisfactory decision for you:

- If you are currently unemployed and not yet fully qualified for a business analysis role, you may find it difficult to get hired into a business analyst job. A transitional job may help you meet your short-term income needs while moving you toward your business analysis career goals.
- If you are currently employed in a role with little or no means for expanding your business analysis experience, seeking a new transitional role in your organization or a new organization may open up new prospects.
- If you do not feel confident in your ability to move directly into a mid-level or senior-level business analyst position, then choosing a transitional role may help you take a measurable step forward.
- If you are a recent college graduate and cannot find a junior-level business analysis role that suits you, then a transitional role may help you build career experiences and move toward your business analysis career goals.

Since it is possible to build business analysis experience without having the business analyst job title, a transitional role may enable you to maintain or grow your current income stream while also accumulating the qualifications you need to become a business analyst. You could seek a transitional job at your current employer or in a new company. In fact, you might already be in one.

While nearly any occupation can lead you to a business analysis role, some occupations enable you to move more rapidly toward your business analyst career goals. Let's go over a set of roles that have relatively easier entry paths, which may be options if you are coming from a role that is very distant from business analysis or are newly entering the job market. At least one or two of these roles may be commensurate with your current qualifications.

Test Analyst: A test analyst is responsible for executing test cases against a software system before it goes live to the business or to customers. Characteristically, a test analyst is not responsible for test planning, and so the job requirements may be rather lenient. If you regularly find problems with software you use every day and can write up a description for that problem in an easy-to-fix way, then you will meet the main requirements.

In a test analyst role, you will gain exposure to software and the project lifecycle. You will put yourself on a path that may lead to a short-term promotion to a quality assurance engineer, which can lead to business analysis.

Project Coordinator / Analyst: A project coordinator assists a project manager in administrating a project. This role involves an extensive range of responsibilities, which is what can make it a straightforward way to work into a business analyst role. You might be collating time sheets, reviewing vendor invoices, capturing meeting notes, and updating project schedules, among other tasks assigned to you by the project manager.

Sometimes the project manager you work for is filling a combined business analysis / project management role, and if they happen to like the business analyst responsibilities the least, they could assign you some actual business analysis tasks.

Administrative Assistant To A CIO, CTO, Or Other Technology Executive: A close relation to the project coordinator is the administrative assistant to a CIO (Chief Information Officer), CTO (Chief Technology Officer), or other technology executive. These roles also involve a broad set of responsibilities, as your tasks will include whatever your executive needs help with on a given day or week.

Responsibilities could range from booking travel to helping prepare presentations for the board of directors. In this role, you may gain a lot of exposure not just to projects but to the executive thinking behind projects, which can serve you well when you are working with higher-level stakeholders as a business analyst.

The challenge with this role is that you might be too busy keeping up with your executive's schedule to carve out time for your own professional development. Also, within your organization you could be typecast into an administrative role, making it difficult to secure an internal promotion to business analysis.

Any Sort Of Analyst: It might seem trite, but getting into *any* role with the term *analyst* in the job title may help you move toward being a business analyst. In fact, given how inconsistently job titles are used, the job might actually be rather close to a business analysis role.

Below are some common example titles and typical responsibilities for different types of analyst roles:

- **Marketing Analyst** ~ Responsible for analyzing the effectiveness of marketing campaigns or generating data that can be used as part of the sales and marketing process.

- **Sales Analyst** ~ Responsible for analyzing sales-related systems, compiling sales reports, conducting customer research, or helping develop sales proposals.

- **Operations Analyst** ~ Responsible for analyzing operational processes, generating reports, or supporting operations by performing manual tasks.

- **Reporting/Data Analyst** ~ Responsible for designing new reports, analyzing data, and running existing reports to refresh the data.

Customer Service Or Technical Support: Customer service and technical support professionals help customers resolve issues and solve problems. First and foremost, individuals in these roles learn how to ask discerning questions and listen to the answers. They repeatedly need to explain difficult technical issues or arcane business rules to customers who would rather not understand them. They also need to solve the immediate problem for the customer.

Sometimes a customer service or technical support professional may get involved in representing the customer to solve more systemic problems, which can lead them into a subject matter expert role.

Subject Matter Expert: A subject matter expert provides specific business, industry, or functional domain knowledge on a project. They usually work closely with the business analyst, being interviewed about what they need and want out of the project and how the process works today. This role may involve reviewing requirements documentation, participating in demos, and conducting or coordinating user acceptance testing.

As you demonstrate your competence as a subject matter expert, you can ask to be assigned more responsibilities on the project team, perhaps taking notes for the business analyst or drafting preliminary documentation.

The challenge with being a subject matter expert is that the term rarely exists as a job title. Subject matter expert is normally a role you step into while you are employed in a different job. So let's consider that set of openings next.

Any Role With Business Analyst Responsibilities Or In A Company With A Business Analysis Practice: While the above list of occupations are specific job titles and roles you might watch out for, any role with a slice of business analysis responsibilities or in an organization that has a business analysis team could provide a path to a business analyst role.

In general, organizations that have a business analysis practice provide the most potential, as you will have a specific type of business analyst job you can work toward, and your knowledge of the stakeholders, systems, and processes will be viewed as an asset should an internal business analysis position open up. But you could also seek out the most process-oriented or technology-oriented role you qualify for and start there.

When evaluating transitional roles, you are ideally looking for roles that are involved in a project or roles that include at least some business analysis responsibilities. A transitional role should definitely provide you with the ability to expand your communication skills and ideally your analysis skills as well.

Choosing a transitional role essentially means making a choice that offers options for expanding your business analysis experiences, as we discussed in Chapter 3.

Below are some common steps to take as part of this path:

- Decide which transitional role or roles represent the best career prospects for you.
- Explore the job market for openings in these roles. Evaluate how your qualifications stack up against the responsibilities required.
- If you are employed, investigate your current organization for transitional roles.
- Craft a resume that highlights your qualifications for the selected transitional role. If you are focusing on more than one type of role, you may need more than one resume.

While we are speaking about these roles as transitional in the context of your business analysis career goals, take care not to use these terms when interviewing for jobs. It is acceptable to be open about your long-term career goals, but if you over-emphasize your long-term goals you may never get hired in the short-term into the role that will help you achieve your long-term goals.

In short, treat a transitional role as a goal in and of itself, and fill it with all the passion and professionalism you intend to bring to your business analysis career. If you are not able to do this, you might consider selecting a different type of transitional role or focusing your energy on the other paths to business analysis.

✓ Putting It To Practice #18

Set A Short-Term And A Long-Term Career Goal

At the end of the last chapter, you answered some questions to define the type of business analyst role you want to move into. In this section, we have discussed three different leaps you can take to move your business analysis career forward. It is time to decide what leaps forward make the most sense for you and if the goal you set is a short-term or long-term goal.

The timeframes for short-term and long-term are relative. Define these in such a way that works well for you. If in doubt, select a time frame of between three and six months for your short-term goal and two to three years for your long-term goal.

- For example, you might decide that you would like to fill a transitional job role in the next three months with the long-term goal of leaping into a mid-level business analyst role in two years.

- Alternatively, you may realize that you are already in a transitional role and can build new business analysis experiences in the short-term, then leap into a mid-level business analyst role a year from now.
- Or, you may realize that you are currently in a mid-level business analyst role and want to move forward into a senior-level business analyst role a few years from now.

The time frames can be flexible, and your goals may change as you learn more. What is important is that you have set a long-term goal that can frame your short-term activities.

Three Ways To Make The Leap A Reality

Now that we have discussed the three leaps forward you might consider making, let's walk through the different ways you can make the leap a reality. In this section, we will discuss internal promotions, establishing new roles, and seeking a new job in a new organization.

Pursue An Internal Promotion

One of the easiest paths into business analysis is to secure an internal promotion simply because your hiring manager will often have first-hand experience of your skills and competencies. Also, success is more probable because you are familiar with the people, tools, and terminology.

If your organization employs professionals in a business analysis role or a transitional role, consider working specifically toward that job. Learn as much as you can about your target roles in your organization. Evaluate job postings, speak to members of the team, and speak to other employees who work with these individuals.

Explore the answers to the following questions:

- Is this role a role that I would enjoy?
- How do my skills and qualifications stack up against the expectations for this role?
- How can I expand my skill set and qualify myself for this role?
- How frequently do new positions open up?
- What backgrounds do individuals newly hired into this position have?

Answering these questions may help you find positions with a clear promotion path as well as find specific training to explore and skill gaps to fill.

Below are some common steps to take as part of this path:

- Evaluate who in your organization has business analysis responsibilities. (Remember, they may or may not have the business analyst job title.)
- Take on new responsibilities that will help close your experience gaps.
- Pursue internal and external training options to expand your skill set.
- Reach out to people filling your target roles to learn more about the role and how people get hired.
- Update your resume to highlight relevant skills and experiences. Prepare to speak to your relevant experiences in a job interview.
- Volunteer to work on any project in which you will interact with business analysts or other employees with business analysis responsibilities.

Being promoted into a business analyst position might not be an option for you because your organization does not have a business analysis role today. That does not mean, though, that your organization does not provide options to become a business analyst. Next we will consider how you can establish a new role that helps move your career forward.

Establish A New Role In Your Current Organization

Nearly any organization can benefit from business analysis, but many organizations do not employ business analysts. If you find yourself working in such an organization, your clearest path into business analysis might be to propose a new business analysis role that you can be hired into. This tactic can work for any type of business analyst role, whether it is general, specialized, or hybrid, and can also work for transitional roles. If your company has a business analysis position, but it is completely misaligned with your career goals, you may be able to propose a different type of business analysis role that is a better fit.

In order to succeed at establishing a business analyst role, there needs to be a clear benefit or problem to be solved by adding business analysis competencies in your organization and enough project or process work to fill the plate of a full-time business analyst. If you can articulate a clear benefit but not find enough work, you may have better luck proposing a hybrid role first.

Before proposing a role, frame the key responsibilities and skill sets for the position, and even consider what type of projects the business analyst would contribute to. Since business analysis roles vary widely across the industry, when defining a role for your organization, it is more important that the skills and responsibilities be perceived as immediately valuable than that they adhere to an ideal vision of a business analyst role you might find elsewhere. Once in a business analyst role, you can always expand your scope of responsibilities.

With your proposed job description prepared, meet with your manager or a manager you think might be receptive to casting such a role on his or her team, and walk through your ideas. Discuss the problems or needs you have seen. Detail how the person filling the business analyst role could solve these problems. Speak to tangible examples of where business analysis activities have already helped demonstrate concrete value in your organization.

Your actions in this step will be better received if you have already begun to incorporate business analysis activities into your work. When your stakeholders can see the impact of business analysis in action, they will be more apt to embrace the idea of someone filling this role on an ongoing basis. As an outcome from this step, you find a manager to establish a new job role on their team. In some less formal organizations, you might begin doing the work before being given a new title or promotion.

In other organizations, the role will be officially established and opened to both internal and external candidates, in which case you will need to apply for it like any other job applicant. You may be competing with other candidates from inside and outside the organization. Update your resume, ready yourself for the job interview, and be prepared to position yourself as qualified and able to fill these new responsibilities. In particular, speak to your experience doing similar business analysis activities in the past for this organization, your knowledge of and relationship with internal stakeholders, and the value of your organizational knowledge and expertise. This is also an advantageous time to share any professional development in which you have participated to grow your own business analysis skills and your intentions for continuing to expand your skill set.

Even if your organization will benefit from increased business analysis competencies, there can be external factors, such as a lack of budget, overwhelming work for your current job, or management resistance, that impact your ability to propose and be positioned in a new internal business analyst role. If your proposal is initially rejected, don't give up, but do keep your eyes open for openings to make your case a second, third, or fourth time while persisting in taking on business analysis job responsibilities.

The best times to re-visit your proposal would be when your organization initiates an major project, an individual filling business analysis responsibilities leaves the company or takes an extended leave, or when your organization begins growing fast and needs to scale its processes to deal with increased customers.

Seek A New Job In A New Organization

If you are unemployed, then to find either a business analysis or transitional role, you will be seeking a new job in a new organization. Finding a new job is also an option if you find yourself in a job with absolutely no potential.

Before giving up on your current organization, it is important to be sure that you are making an informed decision. All too often I see people leave jobs with options instead of doing the tough work to turn possibility into reality. They end up in a new job but in the same situation and do not move any further ahead. These individuals tend to find themselves in one role after another with new hopes of making their career goals a reality and get frustrated because the situation does not turn out like they expect. After a while it becomes more difficult for this person to find a new job because they have switched companies so habitually. The problem is not with the employer. The problem is with their approach. Until they change it, they will not be successful in meeting their career goals.

Below are some situations in which your current company might not be a suitable place to grow your business analysis career:

- The company is shrinking year after year, which means that revenues and/or profits are declining or it is losing market share.
- No investments are made in projects, and no plans are in place to invest in projects. All employee effort is dedicated to supporting existing customers and fixing issues.
- Your company has a pervasive break-fix mentality, which means that leadership waits until something breaks to fix it. You do not see any organizational leaders paving the way to change this culture.

One situation that is not on this list is when project teams are overworked and fail to use business analysis practices. Readers repeatedly e-mail me about situations in which sound business analysis practices are not being applied to their projects, and as a result, teams are rushing to meet critical deadlines and fixing issues in the eleventh hour. They ask if they should leave to find a company with better practices. Business analysis practices are applied inconsistently across organizations. I have seen business analysts change companies for this reason only to find themselves in the same situation or even a worse situation in their new company.

A better approach is to dig in and contribute to projects in any way you can. Focus on solving one project problem at a time and applying any business analysis techniques in your work. Educate your team members, managers, and executive leaders about the value of business analysis. Over time, you may find yourself growing a business analyst role and putting yourself in a position to establish a new role for yourself.

Before deciding to leave an organization, be sure you talk to your manager and at least one other manager in the organization about your business analysis career goals. Volunteer to take on extra responsibilities. Seek out avenues for internal training and mentoring. Invest time outside of work to read books and get involved in the business analysis community. Share these activities with the managers you speak to. If you still do not see a path to at least building business analysis experiences, it may be time to move to a new company to make your career goals a reality.

Provided that you have determined that no options are available to move forward in your current company, then your best bet is to pursue a job in a new company. Start by deciding what types of positions to apply for. Again, you can choose to pursue any type of business analysis role or a transitional role. If you choose a transitional role, you will be searching for a role that opens up the opportunities discussed previously in this chapter. Valuable transitional roles may be in organizations that hire business analysts, promote from within, and have a steady stream of new project investments.

Below are some steps that you can take to prepare for your job search:

- View job postings for business analysis jobs and transitional jobs. Since the term business analyst can bring up a diverse set of job postings, use search terms for specific business analysis skills like elicitation and business requirements documents. Also run job searches for any specialized skills you have. Be sure to explore jobs that do not have the business analyst job title as well. They may have many business analysis job responsibilities.
- Match your qualifications to the roles you find.
- Decide on one or two types of job profiles to focus on in the short-term.
- Update your resume to showcase your qualifications for your selected job profiles. If you select more than one job profile, you may need more than one resume.

With an updated resume, you are ready to apply for positions. Readers and coaching clients often ask me if their resume is good enough. Your resume is good enough if you hear back from people hiring for jobs for which you are reasonably well qualified. Understand that when you are only applying to jobs online, you will not hear back from every company that you apply to, even if your qualifications match those included in the job posting. Leveraging your professional network can help streamline the path to new openings.

As you begin your job search, below are some steps to take:

- Set up saved searches and e-mail alerts at a few job search websites so that they will send you new job openings matching your search criteria on a regular basis.
- Review relevant job postings in detail, paying careful attention to the job qualifications and responsibilities.
- Match the qualifications on your resume to the qualifications and responsibilities on the posting. Wording is important. Tweak your resume to fit the job posting if necessary.
- Determine if anyone in your professional network can help you learn more about the job or introduce you directly to the recruiter or hiring manager.
- Submit your updated resume with a custom cover letter as an application for the job.
- If possible, follow up on your applications.

Job searches can be intensive and ego-busting processes. That is part of the reason that I suggest investing everything you can in making your current job work before pursuing a new job. The last thing you want to do is focus all of your time and energy finding a new role when it could have been better spent investing in the possibilities that were yours for the taking.

That being said, the side benefit of searching for a job is that you will become much more aware of the business analysis job qualifications in your local area and gain a broader perspective of the business analysis profession. You may even learn about concepts and skills that you can bring back to your current organization.

✓ Putting It To Practice #19

Decide On A Short-Term Path

In this section we have discussed three different ways to take the leap to make your goals a reality: pursuing an internal promotion, establishing a new role, and seeking a new job in a new company. One of these ways may well fit for your current situation. Decide on one path that you will work on for the next three to six months.

You might think it is better to pursue multiple paths at once. Focusing on one path in the short-term generates more momentum. If you are simultaneously pursuing more than one path, your time and attention will be divided.

Your decision is not final. Be sure to set a specific date within the next six months when you will re-evaluate your decision. You may also want to establish a specific set of criteria that would trigger you to re-evaluate your decision. For example, if you speak to three managers in your organization about your business analysis career goals and receive an explicitly negative response, then you might choose to invest your future efforts in your job search.

Three Ways To Step Before You Leap

After reading the above, you may discover that now is not the best time for you to tackle a big career move. Perhaps you are in a transitional job role that you enjoy and that is ripe with potential. Perhaps you have a lot going on in your life outside of work and feel that it is best to put your career goals on the back burner for the time being.

Even if taking a big leap forward is not the best decision for right now, you can still move toward your business analysis career goals. Doing so will position you to pursue new openings when the time is right. In this section, we will go through three ways to step forward before you leap: building business analysis experiences, pursuing training, and getting certified.

Build Business Analysis Experiences

As we saw in Chapter 3, it is possible to build additional business analyst experiences even if you are not currently employed as a business analyst. Many business analysts, like Aaron, unconsciously follow this path for several years before realizing that they are well-qualified business analysis professionals. You can make your transition happen more swiftly by consciously seeking out relevant career experiences.

When you follow this path, you want to focus primarily on competency gaps that are most relevant in the business analysis job marketplace. Use the skills assessment you conducted in Chapter 2. Re-visit Putting It To Practice #8, and focus on kicking off a cycle of one business analysis experience leading to another so that you fill in your gaps. Seek out progressively more challenging responsibilities, and work on building your business analysis resume.

One of the advantages of this path is that it is relatively easy to follow. Once you see the possibilities, you are going to find ways to build business analysis experiences and to fill your skill gaps. As long as you are flexible in how you perform business analysis tasks, have quite a bit of time to invest, and follow through on the commitments that you make, you will find occasions to expand your experience.

Below are some common steps to take as part of this path:

- Complete your business analysis skills assessment as outlined in Chapter 2. Determine your areas of strength and skill areas where you would like to practice and gain more experience.
- Use the list of ideas in Chapter 3 to brainstorm ideas to expand your experience.
- Take on one or more business analysis responsibilities. Evaluate what you learned. Repeat.
- With each new experience, update your resume and/or record of business analyst experiences.

You can support this path by investing in some supplemental training. And that's the topic of the next step forward.

Pursue Training

Business analysis training comes in different forms. Pursuing training in business analysis can help you fill specific competency gaps or gain a deeper appreciation for the profession. Remember how Aaron Whittenberger invested in a Business Analyst Bootcamp and then realized that he had been doing many business analysis activities for a long time. Others make a similar investment and then realize new ways to take on business analysis responsibilities. Many course participants originally assume that they will document a fictional process or use case only to find an approach to apply the techniques at work.

With training comes increased awareness and credibility. When you choose to invest in your own training, it sends a clear signal that you are serious about your business analysis career goals. If you can secure organizational funds to cover the investment in training, it is a clear sign that your organization is ready to invest in you.

While training may sometimes be expensive, it does not always have to be. Consider the following types of training programs:

- In-Person Seminars
- Virtual Training Programs
- Professional Meetings
- Professional Conferences
- Study Groups
- Group Mentoring / Coaching
- Individual Mentoring / Coaching
- Formal Education

It is also possible to learn a lot by leveraging the following, many of which are free or low-cost:

- Webinars
- Books
- Online Articles
- Online Forums

Training in the business analysis space can focus on the entire breadth of business analysis or on one or more specific skill sets. If you find yourself having many skill gaps, an end-to-end course in the business analysis essentials will help you get your bearings in the business analysis profession. If, on the other hand, you already have general knowledge of what it takes to be a business analyst but find yourself with specific skill gaps, a more specific course can help you build up your qualifications to meet the demands of the marketplace.

For example, many business analysts who are just getting started lack confidence in putting together a formal requirements specification.

Training in a specific type of specification, such as use cases, business requirements documents, or business process models increases their confidence in performing as a business analyst. Ideally you will apply what you learn right away so you can expand your business analysis experiences as well.

As you pursue training, you will become aware of the certification options open to business analysts. Let's review those next.

Get Certified

Professional certificates or certifications may be effective ways to demonstrate a baseline of knowledge in a field and show your dedication to a profession and to your professional development. Within the business analysis profession, the most common certification is the Certified Business Analysis Professional™ (CBAP®) offered by the International Institute of Business Analysis (IIBA). The IIBA also offers the Certification of Competency in Business Analysis™ (CCBA®). Some training programs also offer certificates.

Before we dive any deeper into your options, let's make a clear distinction between certificates and certifications. IIBA offers certifications. Some training companies (often endorsed education providers by IIBA) offer certificates. When it comes to certification in business analysis, the IIBA options are the logical choice. They validate knowledge against the *BABOK Guide*® and a recipient's relevant experience in business analysis.

A certificate from a training company usually represents participation in one or more courses and, sometimes, that you passed a test. Therefore, these certificates represent knowledge in business analysis. They can be pricey. A certificate will cost you anywhere from $2,000 to $10,000 by the time you pay for all the classes and the extra certificate fees.

Both certificates and certifications can help you position yourself in the business analysis profession. Neither is required nor will obtaining a credential like this guarantee placement in a corresponding job role. If you want to make the investment in a credential as part of meeting your business analysis career goals and meet the work experience requirements to pursue either the CBAP® or CCBA® certifications, the logical choice is to pursue the certification instead of a certificate.

Let's evaluate the CBAP® and CCBA® in a bit more detail. Applying for either the CBAP® and the CCBA® requires that you have a minimum amount of business analysis work experience aligned with *A Guide to the Business Analysis Book of Knowledge* (*BABOK Guide*®), twenty-one professional development hours in the last four years, two references, and that you sign the Code of Conduct. Once your application is accepted, you are able to sit for an exam that tests your knowledge of the *BABOK Guide*®.

The biggest differentiators between the CBAP® and CCBA® are the total amount of work experience required and the overall diversity of your experience.

You may qualify to sit for the CCBA® exam if you can document at least 3,750 hours of work experience aligned with the *BABOK Guide*® in the last seven years. You also must have at least 900 hours in two of the six knowledge areas or 500 hours in four of the six knowledge areas.

In contrast, applying for the CBAP® requires more experience. A minimum of 7,500 hours of business analysis work experience aligned with the *BABOK Guide*® is required in the last ten years. You also must be able to document 900 hours in four of the six knowledge areas.

As we have stressed over and over again in this book, it is possible to have done business analysis work without the business analyst job title. Any work you do that is aligned with the *BABOK Guide*® may be documented as part of your application for either certification. For candidates who have a fair amount of experience but not the job title or formal role, certifications can help boost your credibility. While it is improbably that you will be hired based on having the certification alone, if you find yourself searching for a new job in a new company, either certification could help you be called for an interview.

For a new business analyst, the confidence that comes from documenting your work experience using business analysis terminology can be one of the biggest benefits of getting certified. The knowledge areas cover a broad realm of business analyst activities. It is possible that after going through a study group, reading the *BABOK Guide*®, or taking a formal training class, you will discover that you have been doing business analysis activities under other names for a long time.

Several certifications can augment the CBAP® or CCBA®. These include the Project Management Professional® (PMP®), the Program Management Professional® (PgMP®), the PMI Professional in Business Analysis (PMI-PBA℠), the Certified Business Process Professional® (CBPP®), and assorted agile certifications for Scrum masters and product owners.

Out of all of the possible certifications, the PMP® is by far the most common, and the PMI-PBA℠ is also worth examining. The PMP® is for project managers what the CBAP® is for business analysts. However, unlike the CBAP®, which has yet to become a common job requirement, the PMP® is frequently seen as a de facto requirement for many project management jobs. PMP® recipients exist in droves. There were over 500,000 PMP®-certified professionals as of 2013.

The PMP® has a special place in the business analyst's career path. It is probable that if you are interviewing for a business analyst position, you might be interviewing with a PMP®- certified project manager or with an executive that has several PMP®-certified project managers on their team. Having your PMP® can give you instant credibility when you talk to these people, especially if you are talking about project management concepts. If you are considering a combined role or planning to progress into business analysis management and leadership roles, securing a PMP® in addition to your CBAP® or CCBA® can be a wise career move.

The PMI-PBA℠ was introduced in 2014 and represented PMI's first formal entry into the business analysis space. As of this writing, the certification remains too new to have a large body of recipients, and it is unknown exactly how it will impact the business analysis job market. However, given PMI's stature and reach, it can be expected that the number of recipients and potential recognition commanded by the PMI-PBA℠ will grow quickly.

Again, no certification is essential nor will any of the certifications discussed above guarantee you a path into business analysis. The same is true when it comes to certificates offered by training companies and degrees offered by educational institutions. The primary value in such credentials tends to be in the knowledge gained through training and the professional development hours needed as part of applying for a certification.

Putting It To Practice #20

Brainstorm Action Steps

At this point, you have identified a short-term and long-term career goal and decided which path you will take to move toward that goal. Now it is time to consider the concrete steps you will take to move forward.

Brainstorm a list of possible steps you could take. Use the steps listed in this section as a jumping off point. Be specific. For example, instead of writing down training, write down specific skills in which you need training or specific programs in which you want to invest.

Go back to the previous two sections. You will notice that each section has a list of steps commonly taken as part of pursuing that path. Use these ideas to generate more ideas.

You might feel overwhelmed by everything you could do or feel like you have a lot to do, and it is all important. In the next chapter you are going to take this list of tasks, as well as the other lists you have identified during previous exercises, and turn it into a manageable plan that will help you take immediate action.

CHAPTER

7

Move Toward Your Business Analyst Career Goals

You cannot use your time to the best advantage if you do not make some sort of plan.

~ Eleanor Roosevelt

In the last chapter, we discussed the three leaps forward that you can take, the ways to make those leaps a reality, and the three different ways you can move forward even if now is not the time to make a big leap. Now we will wrap everything together into a plan.

If you have done the exercises so far, you have set a short-term goal and a long-term goal and selected one path to pursue in the short term. You also have some ideas about steps you can be taking even if now is not the time to make a monumental leap.

Now we will discuss what steps to take on your path to your short-term goal. Focusing on a short-term goal makes sense because as you step forward, the options open to you will change. It does not make sense to invest an enormous amount of time planning more than six months or so out. If you follow the advice laid out in this book, your current reality should be different six months from now. Then you can build a new short-term plan for the upcoming three to six months.

But having a long-term goal is still important because you want your short-term goal to move you toward your long-term goal. Without a long-term goal in mind, you risk wandering off in a direction that does not get you where you want to go.

In short, your long-term goal provides context. Your short-term goal generates action.

Define A Plan That Gets You Taking Action Right Now

Let's talk about taking action. This section is especially relevant if you have decided that in the short-term your best strategy is to take small steps while staying exactly where you are today. Having a plan and putting it into action will help you feel more successful even if you are not taking a big recognizable leap.

To get started, pull out all of your notes and worksheets. Pull together anything you have written down or typed up as you went through the exercises in this book. Read through them one time to refresh your memory. If you have not been doing the exercises, then take half an hour or so right now to brainstorm ideas and think about what you might do to move your career forward. At this point, do not limit yourself to your short-term goal. Write down anything that might make sense to do now or in the future. If you get stuck, review the lists of bullet points in the previous chapter with suggested next steps and review the previous exercises.

With your list of ideas in mind, turn your attention again to your short-term and long-term goals. Consider whether they are still the appropriate framework for planning.

- Does your long-term goal represent where you really want to be?
- Does your short-term goal move you toward your long-term goal?
- Does your short-term goal represent a leap forward that excites you?

If you can't answer yes to these questions, re-work your goals so that you can.

Now comes the difficult part. Select between three and five next steps that move you toward your short-term goal. This is difficult because it could be that everything on your list seems important. When you are selecting a handful of tasks, you are choosing not to focus on tasks that seem important for an extended period of time. However, choosing to focus on some tasks and set others aside for the time being is absolutely essential to get you moving. When you have time to take action, you do not want to have to decide what to do. Your plan should be ready to go so you can make the most of any slivers of time you have available to you.

You might easily be able to narrow your list down to between ten and fifteen tasks. Once you have a shorter list, here are some criteria you can run possible tasks against to further winnow down the possibilities:

- Does each task specifically align with my short-term career goal?
- Do any tasks need to be completed after other tasks and therefore should be deferred until those tasks are complete?
- What tasks seem most appealing?
- Is there one task that I really do not want to do but know that I should do? Can I include one challenging item on my list for the next few months?
- What tasks will get me moving forward the fastest?

If you get stuck, realize that you cannot make a wrong decision. Any tasks that get you moving forward are better than no tasks at all. If you get stuck narrowing your focus to the best tasks, it would be better to put your top tasks into a hat and randomly pick three to work on than to invest more than an hour thinking and re-thinking about what to work on. Once you get to work, more clarity will emerge. Re-visit your plan in a week or a month, and make more informed choices.

Once you have narrowed your list to between three and five tasks, you want to define a plan. With the Resource Pack, I have included a worksheet that walks you through this. (You may download the Resource Pack for free by visiting the following link: http://www.bridging-the-gap.com/ba-resource-pack.)

For each task, write down the following:

- Re-phrase the task so it is specific and actionable. Will you know when it is complete? For example, *update resume* is a decent draft, but it is not very specific. *Craft a resume that's ready to send to recruiters by next Tuesday* is better.
- Identify why the task is important and how it moves you toward your short-term goal.
- Prioritize each task so you know what to work on first.
- Set a target completion date for the task.

That's it. With your short list of tasks, it is time to get to work.

One thing you might realize in completing this planning exercise is that your short list of tasks does not actually add up to achieving your short-term goal, even though completing the tasks might consume the time in which you want to achieve your short-term goal. If this happens, either your short-term goal is too aggressive, or you have selected the wrong tasks.

This can be an insightful reality check to make sure that you are working on the most important tasks and not deferring the seemingly difficult work that will move your career forward. When this happens, you can either adjust your short-term goal to be a reflection of your tasks or adjust your tasks to meet your short-term goal.

Putting It To Practice #21

Define A Plan To Achieve Your Short-Term Goal And Get Moving!

The time to get moving is now! Invest an hour stepping through the planning approach outlined above, and then work your plan. Again, the Resource Pack includes a worksheet that will walk you step-by-step through this process.

(And if this planning approach does not work for you, feel free to use your own method. But whatever you do, select a high-priority task and get to work!)

Action generates results.

Stay Open To New Opportunities

While it is important to have a plan so you do not waste valuable time thinking and re-thinking when you should be taking action, it is equally important to be open to new opportunities. Your plan should not restrict you from taking advantage of the possibilities that life throws your way. For example, you may decide that it makes sense to defer updating your resume right now and instead focus on building more business analysis experiences. Then you might meet a recruiter who has a position open that is a superb fit for your qualifications. If you stick to your plan, you will miss acting on the opening. So change your plan.

You might make adjustments to your next steps, re-prioritize your tasks, and adjust your commitment dates. In fact, if you do not find yourself making these sorts of changes, you probably are not staying aware of the fortunes coming your way. Expect your plan to change, and flow with the changes.

One challenging aspect of opportunity is that it is not something you can directly control or plan for. I did not control the timing of my senior editor's three week vacation, when a new business analyst role opened up in my company, or the referral that I received to a new business analyst role in a new company. Each of these things happened when they happened, and I jumped on the chances when they did.

Once you move in the direction of your business analysis career goals, your world will shift, and possibilities will open up for you. It is impossible to anticipate how these shifts will happen in advance, so you must be ready to deal with them as they happen. This is why I recommend such a light planning process that only projects ahead a few months. It is less important that you develop a perfect plan and more important that you take concrete steps forward, stay open to new possibilities, and re-visit your plan regularly.

When an opportunity presents itself, it is important to act. Even if you feel overwhelmed by the challenge, trust yourself to figure it out. If you spend too much time thinking about whether the break is the right one before you take action, your chance may slip away. When in doubt, step up. It is almost always better to accept a challenge than not to. Preparing ahead of time can help. Learn everything possible. Connect with other business analysis professionals so you have a list of people you can draw on for assistance. Practice if you can.

Most often, when people do not take opportunities, it is because they fear failure. They work and plan and prepare, but then the door opens, and they do not walk through it. As analysts, we tend to over-think decisions, under-estimate our abilities, and want to be so prepared that failure is impossible. We set unreasonably high standards for what we believe to be a successful outcome. All of these mindsets keep us from acting.

If you do miss an opportunity, it is not the end of the world. It is a minor failure that you can learn from. Examine why you stepped back from the chance, and use this new knowledge to be better prepared for the next opening. But do not side-step too many opportunities, or you will slow down your momentum and make your path more difficult than it needs to be.

How To Gain Momentum

Career transitions are difficult, as is any sort of big career change or life change. We naturally resist change. While in this book we are doing everything we can to help clear your path and break down roadblocks for you, that does not mean that you can avoid hard work and that there will not be any roadblocks for you to overcome. Before this book comes to an end, let's have a frank discussion about how to get moving and stay moving.

This Is A Journey, Not A Destination

The first thing to realize is that your career change is a journey, not a destination. I struggle with this concept every day. I get so set on specific goals, specific milestones, and specific achievements that sometimes I forget about the path that I am on, and I forget to take time to smell the roses along the way.

What this concept means is that we need to appreciate the journey almost as much as we appreciate achieving our career goals. This means that we are proud of the steps we take, no matter how trivial they might seem to us, and that we take time to celebrate the slightest of successes.

Enjoying the journey also means that we find fulfillment in the act of making change happen. Each step, from updating your LinkedIn profile to volunteering to take notes in a meeting, is a moment to relish.

It means that even when you do something scary, such as go on a job interview or introduce yourself to the president of your local IIBA chapter, you find pleasure in the process and enjoy the chance to put your best foot forward.

Of course, there will be tasks that you would rather not do. While you might get excited about the first three drafts of your resume, completing the final nuts and bolts and editing review may be something that you would rather put off to another day. It is natural not to love every moment of the journey and to avoid the more challenging work that needs to be done.

But, in general, the things that you do not like about this journey should be the exception rather than the rule. If you study your plan and it makes you unhappy, or it represents a set of things in which you just do not want to invest your time, it might be telling you something about your goal itself or about how you have chosen to approach your goal. It is time to adjust.

Take Small Steps

Do not let this last statement give you an out from achieving what you really want to achieve. Unhappy is different than uncomfortable, which is a sign of fear. You will feel uncomfortable at times. But once you get through what is making you uncomfortable, you should feel fulfillment in what you have just achieved.

This brings me to a very important concept: the concept of small steps. In a book called *One Small Step Can Change Your Life: The Kaizen Way*, Robert Maurer tells a story of a woman who goes to the emergency room and is severely unhealthy. She needs to lose weight. She has been told to diet and exercise a dozen times by different doctors. She is exhausted. She works full-time, and she is a single mother.

The latest doctor chooses a different approach. Instead of repeating the same advice, the doctor recommends that she march in place for one minute a night in front of the television. She is surprised, but she smiles because she feels that she can follow the doctor's advice. One week later, she is back asking the doctor what else she can do in a minute. The doctor gives her another one-minute exercise. Within months, she is doing full aerobic exercises of her own volition, and her key health statistics are moving in the right direction.

From this story, we learn that small steps lead to bigger leaps. When you think about a big goal like starting a career as a business analyst, it might be so overwhelming that it stops you in your tracks. Some of the work you will need to do is going to involve stepping outside of your comfort zone and will make you feel uncomfortable.

Even choosing three tasks to move you toward your short-term goal might be too much. If you get stuck in this way, step back and ask yourself what you could do in just a few minutes each day and take action. This approach works because while big goals set off our inner-fear alarm bells, small steps, so minor that they are seemingly inconsequential, side-step our inner fears. Steps that are almost underwhelming in terms of their scale guarantee that we can make forward progress. And one step leads to another, which leads to another and another.

If you review this entire book, you will see that the concept of small steps is built in. If you have been doing the exercises, you have been taking steps forward with each chapter. If you have not or still feel stuck, break them down even further into five minute tasks that it is almost impossible for you not to do.

Let's look at an example of how you can make this work. Let's say that one of your tasks is to publish your LinkedIn profile, but you cannot seem to get going. This week set a goal to spend five minutes a day reviewing other people's LinkedIn profiles. Next week, perhaps, you could simply register and enter a few pieces of information into an unpublished profile. Maybe you continue to invest five minutes a day adding to that profile all week. Before long, you will have seen what the LinkedIn profile can do for you, and you will probably be ready to publish it. But do not worry if you are not. Persist in finding something underwhelming to do each day to work on the LinkedIn profile until you are ready to publish it.

Let's consider one more example. Let's say that the idea of volunteering to take on a business analyst responsibility paralyzes you. Instead of volunteering, invest five minutes each day practicing what you would say when you volunteer, reading an article about the responsibility you would like to take on, or visualizing yourself doing the task. Then you might practice the technique without showing anyone your work. Keep taking steps until you are ready to perform the work publicly.

The important thing is that you keep moving, no matter how inconsequential your steps might seem. Of course, if you are speeding along in your plan and fear is not in your way, by all means keep going. Do not step back and take small steps. But as soon as you feel at a loss, or you find yourself deferring something you know you should do, stop and set a less daunting goal to get moving again.

Check In On Your Progress Regularly

Another tactic that will help you get moving and stay moving is to review your task list regularly and track your progress. As suggested by David Allen in *Getting Things Done*, I conduct weekly reviews to plan out my next actions against all of my important personal and business projects. Regular progress checks and tactical planning ensures that you are investing your most limited asset, your time, in such a way that propels you toward your career goals.

As you track your progress, be sure to celebrate any tasks you complete. If you update your resume, publish your LinkedIn profile, or take on a new responsibility, celebrate it. Pat yourself on the back, share your story with a friend, or treat yourself to something special.

This might seem dorky, but it works, and it will help you keep your momentum going.

One reader shared a story about how she volunteered to work on a project and had been assigned new business analysis responsibilities. Initially she was bubbling over with excitement. Then she thought about her long-term goal of starting a business analyst career and became frustrated. She saw what she did not yet have. She was not in a business analyst role, she did not have the business analyst job title, and her project was not nearly as noteworthy as what she wanted to do in the future. Negative thoughts squashed her enthusiasm. However, that week, I happened to publish an article about celebrating your successes, no matter how trivial. She realized that she had every reason to celebrate her new responsibilities. Taking on these tasks represented a wonderful milestone in her career. She decided to own her success and celebrate her achievements.

This is the value of checking in on your progress. If you do not evaluate what you are doing, you might not see the progress you are making, and you might let your frustration about not achieving your longer-term career goals supersede your excitement about your forward progress.

Re-visit Your Plan

In addition to taking small steps and checking in on your progress, make sure you are keeping the big picture in mind. That means that you need to re-visit your plan on a regular basis.

Set an appointment in your calendar to re-visit your tasks in the next three to six months. Better yet, if you finish all of the tasks on your list, then use the same process to formulate a new plan at that time.

When you review your plan, contemplate the entire picture. Review your short-term and long-term career goals and make sure they still make sense. Revise them if they do not. New information or opportunities may have come up that could necessitate amending your goals. You may need to set a new short-term goal because you have already achieved the one you started with. Then select between three and five steps to take to move toward your new short-term goal, and repeat the planning process we walked through above.

Focus On What You Can Control

As you go through the planning process and take action to move your career forward, you will realize that some aspects of starting your business analyst career are outside of your direct control. You cannot control your manager's response to your proposal to incorporate a new business analysis role in your organization, you cannot control a recruiter's decision whether to bring you in for an interview, and you cannot control the projects your organization decides to invest in this year. But you can control the type of role you propose, how well you prepare for a job interview, and what tasks you volunteer for.

One of the most challenging aspects of this journey will be focusing on what you can control and working around what you cannot control. Another way to phrase this is that it is quite possible that you will face rejection somewhere along your path that has nothing to do with you personally. While you can take many steps independently, achieving your career goals will at some point require that someone else make a decision in your favor.

Many decisions are constrained by budgets, accepted practices, and information that you might not be privy to. The recruiter might know about a special skill required for a job that he never shares with you, and your manager may want to establish a role for you but not have the budget to do it. The people who succeed do not let these setbacks get to them personally. They learn what they can from every setback and use it to move forward in a new way. If you keep persisting in this way, you will find success.

When you experience a setback, whether it be something considerable, like not getting an important project assignment, or something less consequential, like not hearing back when you submit your resume for a job posting, do your best to learn from the experience. Explore what you could do differently next time. Learn without self-blame. Focus on what you can control: your actions, your knowledge, and the way you communicate. Allow the fact that this particular prospect did not materialize roll off of you so that you are prepared to embrace the next one. Do not allow yourself to develop assumptions and patterns that keep you from pursuing success. If business analysis is a suitable fit for you, and if you keep pursuing your best options going forward, you will find success.

The people who succeed do not wallow in every mistake, but neither do they resign their fate to an outside force that they cannot control. While it might initially seem that everyone who is successful is a different age than you, has a different special skill, or the perfect career background, the reality is that business analysts come from all ages, specializations, and backgrounds. Yes, there will be specific openings that do not work out for any one or all of these reasons, but they are not over-arching forces that will forever keep you from achieving your career goals. If it seems that you face resistance at every turn, explore ways around, over, or through your roadblock.

You generate your own career momentum. You can control what you offer, how prepared you are, and what breaks you lean into. You cannot control the chances you have and other people's decisions. Focus on what you can control, and the opportunities will follow, and you will be ready to jump on them when they do.

✓ Putting It To Practice #22

Establish Triggers To Keep Your Momentum Going

It is so easy to get knee deep into your career transition plan, get stuck, and forget about everything you read in the previous section. It may be helpful to chart a few triggers to remember to apply these practices.

Below are some ideas:

- Schedule an appointment in your calendar to re-evaluate your plan in three months.
- Schedule an appointment in your calendar to review your plan and tasks each week. Decide what specific steps you will take in the next week to move toward your goals.
- Brainstorm some ideas for celebrating your accomplishments. Better yet, next to each task on your plan, write down specifically how you will celebrate finishing the task.
- Go through each of your tasks and goals. Determine what you can control to make your goals happen. Determine what is outside of your control.
- List opportunities that you would want to seize if they popped up. Brainstorm ways for increasing their likelihood and preparing to act on them.

If at any time you find yourself lost, review this chapter for ideas about how to get moving. Getting stuck is the most natural thing in the world. It is the people who get unstuck quickly who find the most success.

Conclusion

We have covered the role of the business analyst, the skills you need to be successful as a business analyst, and various ways to expand your business analyst experiences, regardless of the role you are in right now. We moved on to consider how to connect with other business analysis professionals, which can be a time-consuming but also immensely valuable process that will accelerate your advancement within the profession. We finished our discussion with a look at the many different types of business analyst job profiles that are available, the different leaps and steps you can take to move your career forward, and how to create an action plan.

As I mentioned in the beginning, you will get the most out of your investment in this book if you work through the Putting It To Practice exercises. They are designed to help you take the guidance inside this book and apply it to your own career development.

Thank you for embarking upon this journey. I believe in business analysts, and I am excited about the impact that you will make in this profession. I have seen minor changes to the business analysis practice transform teams. I have seen people become happier in their work because they have found a shared definition of success. And, most importantly, I have been fortunate to witness many professionals increase their economic stature, personal confidence, and fulfillment at work by dedicating themselves to the business analysis profession.

You have chosen a profession in which you can make an enormous positive impact. Our profession needs more excellent business analysts. Great business analysts are committed to positive change, making things happen, and creating collaborative work environments.

Business analysis is expanding as a profession, and business analysts will continue to advance how organizations generate value now and in the future. As business analysts get better, the world gets better.

If you have found that business analysis is not the right career path for you, I respect that decision. We all deserve to find fulfillment in profitable careers. I sincerely wish you all the best in discovering the right path and finding the resources to help you along your way.

But if business analysis is the right career path for you, I celebrate the decision that you have made to commence your journey. I am here personally to assist you with getting started and finding your inner confidence as a business analyst so that you can help your organization progress. I offer additional books that explore other business analysis career topics and a variety of courses and coaching services to fit just about any budget.

Many of our readers tell me that during their transition they carry this book with them and refer back to it daily. With each exercise you complete and each step you take, you will learn something new. While no one can do your work for you, you will find a lot of support to assist you along your path. The business analysis profession is full of talented and giving professionals who want to see everyone rise and move forward. You have found a profession full of energy and passion for making the world a better place, one process, one system, and one person at a time.

Thank you for joining the business analysis profession. I send the best of all possible wishes to you as you begin this exciting career adventure!

References

Beal, Adriana. 2010. *Measuring the Performance of Business Analysts.* [E-book available at http://www.bridging-the-gap.com/measuring-the-performance-of-business-analysts/]

Blais, Steven. 2012. *Business Analysis: Best Practices for Success.* Hoboken, NJ: Wiley.

Brennan, Kevin. 2009. *A Guide to the Business Analysis Body of Knowledge®* (BABOK® Guide). Toronto: International Institute of Business Analysis.

Cockburn, Alistair. 2000. *Writing Effective Use Cases.* New York: Addison-Wesley.

Cohn, Mike. 2004. *User Stories Applied: For Agile Software Development.* New York: Addison-Wesley.

Gottesdiener, Ellen and Mary Gorman. 2012. *Discover to Deliver: Agile Product Planning and Analysis.* Boston: EBG Consulting.

Leffingwell, Dean. 2007. *Scaling Software Agility: Best Practices for Large Enterprises.* Boston: Pearson Education.

Lore, Nicholas. 1998. *The Pathfinder: How to Choose or Change Your Career for a Lifetime of Satisfaction and Success.* New York: Fireside.

Kroll, Per and Philippe Kruchten. 2003. *The Rational Unified Process Made Easy: A Practioner's Guide to the RUP.* Boston: Pearson Education.

Maurer, Robert. 2004. *One Small Step Can Change Your Life: The Kaizen Way.* New York: Workman.

Poppendieck, Mary and Tom Poppendieck. 2003. *Lean Software Development: An Agile Toolkit.* New York: Addison-Wesley.

Reis, Eric. 2011. *The Lean Startup: How Today's Entrepreneurs Use Continuous Innovation to Create Radically Successful Businesses.* New York: Crown Business.

Sandberg, Sheryl. 2013. *Lean In: Women, Work, and the Will to Lead.* New York: Random House.

Acknowledgments

My heart is full of gratitude to everyone who made this book possible. First and foremost, every reader or course participant who has ever asked me a question has taught me exactly what was needed in this book and helped me clarify my thoughts and recommendations. Those who have embarked upon this journey before you, and sought my encouragement, have helped ensure that this second edition is clearer, more actionable, and more specific.

A work like this would not be possible without there being a profession of business analysts, a profession full of too many people to list individually, but talented individuals who are fun to work with and demand excellence. You keep me on my toes and help me do my best work. Thank you.

But I did not participate in this journey alone. I was fortunate to have a wonderful support team. Paulette Kinnes helped me delineate my thoughts and make the text more readable. Nick Zelinger brought visual life to the words and the organization you find here. Jen Weers made the elements inside the book findable through a comprehensive and cross-referenced index.

There are many people whose contributions were less direct but whose impact was immense. Specifically, Gary Barnes, my coach, helped me more confidently give to others. Also, Marci Dahms and her team at Indigo Administrative Services efficiently and effectively handled so many of the details involved with running the *Bridging the Gap* business, enabling me to give my time and attention to teaching, writing, and creating. Finally, I acknowledge my husband David Brandenburg for never losing patience with me talking about my writing and business analysis.

About the Author

Laura Brandenburg, CBAP is a best-selling author and an internationally recognized leader known for helping mid-career professionals start business analysis careers. Laura brings more than a decade of experience in the business analysis profession, filling such roles as a full-time business analyst, consultant, and hiring manager. She brings all of these perspectives into her writing, presenting, coaching, and training to help you find transferable business analysis skills, expand your business analysis experience, and begin your business analysis career with confidence. You may find out more about Laura by visiting her website (www.bridging-the-gap.com).

Index

D

E

F

G

H

I

J

K

L

M

N

O

P